Writing Up Your Action Res

Many practice-based researchers have expert knowledge of doing research but often experience difficulties when writing it up and communicating the significance of what they have done. This book aims to help bridge the gap. Packed with practical advice and strong theoretical resources, it takes you through the basics of designing and producing your text so that it will meet established standards and high quality assurance expectations.

The book is divided into three distinct parts, and key points include:

- understanding writing practices;
- engaging with the literatures;
- how to write up a project report or dissertation;
- how writing is judged in terms of professional and academic writing practices;
- developing ideas for further study and publication.

Writing Up Your Action Research Project is an essential text for practitioners on professional education and undergraduate courses across disciplines who want their writing to reflect the excellence of their research. It is the ideal companion to the author's *You and Your Action Research Project*, now in its fourth edition.

Jean McNiff is Professor of Educational Research at York St John University, UK. She also holds visiting professorial positions at Beijing Normal University and Ningxia Teachers University, People's Republic of China, and Oslo and Akershus University College, Norway. She has written widely on action research and professional education.

Jean also offers writing workshops and support on doing and writing practice-based research across disciplines and professions. She can be contacted at jeanmcniff@mac.com and through her website at www.jeanmcniff.com.

Writing Up Your Action Research Project

Jean McNiff

Routledge
Taylor & Francis Group

LONDON AND NEW YORK

First published 2016
by Routledge
2 Park Square, Milton Park, Abingdon, Oxon OX14 4RN

and by Routledge
711 Third Avenue, New York, NY 10017

Routledge is an imprint of the Taylor & Francis Group, an informa business

British Library Cataloguing-in-Publication Data
A catalogue record for this book is available from the British Library

Library of Congress Cataloging in Publication Data
A catalog record for this book has been requested

ISBN: 978–1–138–82831–5 (hbk)
ISBN: 978–1–138–82832–2 (pbk)
ISBN: 978–1–315–73849–9 (ebk)

Typeset in Palatino
by Florence Production Ltd, Stoodleigh, Devon

Printed and bound in Great Britain by
Ashford Colour Press Ltd, Gosport, Hampshire

Contents

Illustrations

FIGURES

TABLES

Acknowledgements

Thanks are due to many people involved in the writing of this book.

First, thanks to all colleagues who are happy to have their works reproduced here. Books get written and new directions forged through the power of working together. Thanks to all.

Then, thanks to Philip Mudd at Routledge Education, for his encouragement, friendship and kindness over the years. Thanks also to the editorial and production staff for the hard work of putting it all together.

And thanks to Peter, the nicest companion anyone could wish for. Lucky me.

Let the words of my mouth, and the meditation of my heart, be acceptable in thy sight, O Lord, my strength, and my redeemer.

Psalm 19:14

Introduction

This book is about writing up your action research project. It is written for practitioners across disciplines, professions and work contexts who are studying on professional education courses, on work-based learning courses and on undergraduate and postgraduate programmes, including for master's degrees. The book is also written for lecturers and tutors delivering these courses. Advanced scholars, too, may find it useful as a core foundation text.

It is the second of two books. The first, *You and Your Action Research Project* (McNiff, 2016), is about doing an action research project: it outlines the 'what, who, when, where, which, how and why' of doing action research. This second book, the one you are reading, is about writing up the action research project described in the first book: it outlines the 'what, who, when, where, which, how and why' of writing. Both books are about researching your practices in action. The first is about researching your practice as a nurse, a builder or an engineer; the second is about researching your practice as a writer. Learning to write becomes an action enquiry within a broader action enquiry.

Many people often do not appreciate the importance of writing as a practice that may be researched in itself: some see it as an add-on, something done after the event. They also assume that the writing will somehow just happen, which is seldom the case. Good-quality writing involves developing specific knowledges, capacities and skills. Further, you write from the first moment you begin a project. Learning to write well is essential to your success and to having your work taken seriously. This is important: you can do the most excellent action research project in the world, but, unless you communicate it appropriately, your reader may not appreciate what you have done, so possibly will not take your work seriously. Therefore, if you feel your writing could be improved, you have to work at it and learn how to do it better.

This is where some people begin to experience doubts: they say, 'I am not a writer: I cannot write'. This is never the case: everyone can write, and write well, provided they put in some effort and learn how to do it. You can do this too; success does involve effort, but it is perfectly achievable. It means studying your practice as a writer and finding ways to improve it. This means that you study two aspects of your practice at the same time. First you ask, 'How do I improve my practice as a nurse, or a builder, or an engineer?', and, at the same time, you ask, 'How do I improve my practice as a writer?' Your desk becomes a research context as much as your other workplace contexts.

Yet this is where things can become tricky. If you are registered on a higher education course, you are by default writing in a higher education context. This means you have to produce writing that will count as good-quality writing in a general sense and, more specifically, as good-quality academic writing. Further, higher education has specific rules and regulations about what counts as academic writing, so you have to learn what the rules are and how to work with them in order to achieve an appropriate quality for your work and ensure that it will be accepted.

This raises another dilemma. You are doing an action research project, so you are writing in a way that is appropriate for an action research approach but is not necessarily appropriate for a conventional academic context. Action research is a work-based, dynamic form of research that welcomes first-person ('I' and 'we') forms of writing, lives happily with contradiction, and does not expect concrete outcomes. Yet this dynamic kind of research is often not accepted in higher education contexts that are premised on conventional scientific/social scientific ideas about what doing research involves. Most higher education institutions tend to think in traditional scientific ways: they assume that research projects will achieve a specific outcome, and that events will follow each other in a 'what next?' order. They therefore tend to want texts that reflect these 'what next?' ways of thinking and action. It is assumed that ideas and chapters, like the research action, will follow each other in a reasonably direct way and will be tightly structured, all neat and tidy, with established section headings, and they will be written in straight lines, not in the curved forms and complex shapes that reflect most action research practices and, indeed, real life.

So – if this organic approach is not always accepted, what to do? Given that you have to accept the rules of the accrediting institution if you want its degree, and given that getting the degree usually involves producing a text for assessment, you have to know what will count as an appropriate text and how to produce one. It is a question of both learning how to produce a text of such quality that it will stand on its own in any arena, and also learning, as necessary, how to fit a dynamic action research report about a dynamic process into the tight, fixed structures of traditional social sciences forms of writing. This means understanding the rules of academic writing and adapting your work so that you find a balance between orthodoxy and innovation.

This, then, becomes a subtle political process: you learn how to work with traditionalist writing structures so that the structures themselves become malleable and begin to bend in your direction. And it is evident that this process is happening around the world: significant numbers of action research texts, including work-based reports, master's dissertations and doctoral theses, have now been accepted by the Academy and placed in the public domain; this is an important factor in the legitimisation of action research and its dynamic forms of writing. Further, success tends to generate success: the more action research texts are accepted into the existing body of knowledge (the canon), the more new accounts are likely to be accepted.

This legitimisation of action research is further helped by the many opportunities that now exist for making your work public and disseminating it through the use of web technologies and, where appropriate, through open-access forms of publication as well as through established forms. These multimodal, multimedia forms of representation can often communicate the dynamic nature of action research better than traditional print-based forms. Further, they require higher education institutions to rethink what counts as a legitimate academic text. New writing and accreditation cultures are emerging where performance and live art are included in academic reports (Butler-Kisber, 2010), and academic staff themselves are agitating for more contemporary forms of representation. The situation is resonant of Graff's (2003) comments. He said that, in the past, universities have frequently complained that students are not ready for university, whereas today the situation is reversed, in that universities are often not ready for their students, who are worldly-wise, technologically savvy and aware of their rights as consumers. Universities themselves need to get their act together if they are to meet the needs of this new clientele, who know what they need in order to get a degree and know how to get it.

This book is one of the resources that will help you to get it. The aim is to offer practical advice and theoretical frameworks that will help you to write up your action research project, get your credits and make your original contribution to knowledge of the field.

This leads to appreciating what researching writing involves.

RESEARCHING WRITING

Researching writing is a fascinating but under-theorised area, nowhere more so than in the higher education contexts of real-world, person-centred forms of research, including action research. The field needs strong practical and theoretical resources that will help practitioners to study writing as a practice, work out how they can improve their own writing practices and put their own theories of writing practices into the field so that others can learn with and from them.

Note, however, that when speaking about theories of writing practices it is important to appreciate that ideas about theory are themselves contested. Traditionalists tend to think of theory as a set of principles that certain people, usually academics and other intellectual elites, draw up and write into books and papers. Much of this work is conducted in the head, and theory itself is often understood as existing in the head or on paper, in an abstract form. It is further assumed that the job of these elites is to think and theorise, whereas the job of 'ordinary', work-based practitioners is to apply those theories to their practices. However, these assumptions have been actively challenged for a century or so and in some contexts are fading from view, as in, for example, the literatures of work-based learning (as in Raelin, 2008; Helyer, 2015). It is now widely recognised that all practitioners, regardless of context, can generate their own theories of practice, and that these are practical theories, embedded in real-world practices. Through an ongoing process of acting and reflecting on the action, and acting again and reflecting again, people can develop deeper understandings of what they are doing. Theorising then becomes a process of the interaction between head and hand. When you create a paper aeroplane, you think carefully as you fold the paper this way and that; equally, when you create a practice, or a life, you think carefully as you try doing things this way and that. You think about what you are hoping to do (a thinking, design-and-planning phase), try it out (an action phase), see if it works (an evaluation phase) and continue in the same way or differently, depending on the results of your evaluation (a revising/rethinking phase). This becomes an ongoing research process where you reach ever more refined levels of analytical capacity and theorising. It is not a split between head and hand, between conceptual and practical theory, but more a combination, a necessary unity of both, as Bateson (2002) would say.

These ideas are especially relevant to the practice of researching writing practices. Researching writing becomes an elegant symbiosis between head and hand, where you think about what you are doing as you do it and come up with new ideas that help you improve what and how you write. Writing becomes its own field that you continually expand through the practice of writing itself.

A useful way to understand how these things work is to think about the idea of conceptual spaces, a term adapted from the work of Gärdenfors (2004), who used it as a metaphor for representing different kinds of information, used in this book to refer to the spaces in your head or mind. You can have a head space where you think about what your text will look like (this is a design space, where you think about design and planning); another where you think about what you will write (this is a production space, where you produce content for your text); and another where you think about how you are going to say it (a communications and analysis space, where you speak to other people and explain why you should speak in a particular way). You can move from one space into another, across and around your head, from designing to producing to communicating to explaining. Also, although these spaces are sequential, in that one leads into the other over time, they are not saltatory, in the sense that one stops and the other begins. Rather, they are transformational, so that design expands into and is embedded within production, which in turn expands into and is embedded within communication, rather like ever-widening concentric circles that move towards ever-expanding horizons (Figure I.1).

You can therefore think of your writing process as designing and producing a text within a broader framework of communicating with your reader and explaining to them what you are doing and why you are doing it this way. This process of explaining why you are doing what you are doing becomes a process of theorising your practice as a writer.

Now, consider also that, in a sense, all writing is done for a reader, even when that reader is yourself. You write (you put marks on a surface such as a page or a screen) so that you can see in an explicit form and at

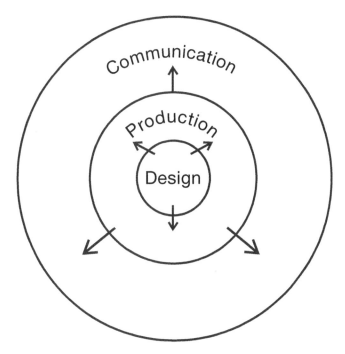

Figure 0.1 Design transforms into communication

an externalised level what is already there in an implicit form and at an internalised level. Writing a report or dissertation usually involves working at these two levels: you first work out ideas for yourself and then begin to make the ideas explicit. Meanings begin to emerge above the surface, into public view. You increasingly make explicit everything that is implicit, thereby explaining more and more what you are doing. By the time you produce a text, in the form of an assignment or dissertation, you are at the point where you are no longer writing here inside for yourself, but are putting your writing out there for a reader.

These, then, are some of the contents and aims of the book. Now, let me set out my reasons for writing it.

MY REASONS FOR WRITING THE BOOK

I have many reasons for writing the book. Some are to do with the idea of celebrating talent and creativity, and others are to do with combating unfairness. First, think about talent and creativity.

Talent and creativity

Everyone, without exception, is talented and creative. If you look at the microscopic organisms that you see on television screens, you will observe the amazing complexity of their structures and functions. If an organism as tiny as the tiniest fly can be made up of millions of complex processes, then how much greater is the complexity of the human body–mind? We humans can process information and make connections faster and more efficiently than any computer, while using only a fraction of our brains at any one time. According to Habermas (1975), we cannot *not* learn in processes of social evolution. In my view, we cannot *not* think at any point in our lives. We are by nature creative: every time we say or write something, we do it for the first time. Further, life is always in a process of evolution: each moment is a new moment, the end of the past and the beginning of the future. Each moment holds its past and future already within itself. It is our choice what to do with this moment and, by implication, how we shape the future.

Appreciating the wonder of these evolutionary processes, however, requires a specific form of thinking, which is open, dynamic and evolutionary, sees relationships and connections in everything, and actively seeks out what Bateson (1972) calls 'the patterns that connect'. Different authors in different domains write about these matters: Boden (1992) explains the creative nature of our thinking; Chomsky (1986) speaks about the evolutionary nature of language acquisition and use; Mitroff and Linstone (1993) speak about the need for innovative and creative thinking in business; Nonaka and Takeuchi (1995) do the same in relation to organisational development. Bergson (1911/1998) speaks about the evolutionary nature of living, whereas Todorov (1990) speaks about the evolutionary nature of stories. Popper (1945) emphasises the need for an open society and for resistance to closure, and so on. My own thinking about these matters was inspired by the work of Spinoza (see, for example, his 1996) and Goethe (see, for example, his 1957), both of whom I studied for my undergraduate studies in German, and later by the work of Chomsky, in my master's studies in applied linguistics. I do not see the world or life as fixed or static, but as in a constant process of dynamic evolution, where everything is connected with everything else, in what Capra (1996) calls 'a web of life'.

Nor do I see a life of social interactions as organised into hierarchies. An evolutionary form of thinking is non-hierarchical and does not work in fragmented ways. It also does not work in terms of looking for closure or final answers, as do conventional scientific ways of thinking. This dynamic, open way of thinking leads me to resist closed forms of thinking that allocate people to different places within artificially constructed hierarchies. Such ways of thinking can act as the basis for unfair practices. This leads to the second main reason why I am writing this book, which is about combating unfairness.

Combating unfairness

A good deal of unfairness is evident everywhere in the world, including in the field of knowledge and knowledge production. It is assumed that some people know things and others do not. Although this may be the case in terms of a lot of subject knowledge (I know a good deal about educational research, but virtually nothing about car maintenance), it is not necessarily the case in terms of the capacity to know or come to know, that is, the capacity to learn. However, this capacity is frequently compromised by circumstances of birth or opportunity. Like many others, I am enormously privileged to live and work in contexts that have enabled me to learn and have confidence in my knowledge. The situation in the world is, of course, that countless millions do not have the opportunity to learn, and even fewer are able to choose to learn.

A good deal of unfairness is also evident in the field of academic work. For me, the term 'academic' is a job description for someone who works in higher education (in the Academy), in the same way as the term 'machinist' is the job description of someone who works with machines. The job description 'academic' is not, as some would believe, a licence to position oneself as superior in knowledge or life status to other so-called practitioners, such as shopkeepers or builders. We are all practitioners: we all work for a living, have job descriptions and are accountable to managers (many of whom wrongly consider themselves superior to others).

Further, the unfairness extends to how research should be done and how its findings should be communicated. It is widely held in conventional research communities that scientific and social scientific research is superior to work-based, practice-based forms of research, and that scientific and social scientific forms of writing are 'correct'. I challenge this view throughout this book and argue that all kinds of research are appropriate for different purposes, according to the real-life contexts of researchers, who are also in relationships where it should be understood that all are of equal status and life worth.

Unfairness is, sadly, also evident in the field of action research, from two directions, from within and from without:

- from within: the field of action research is becoming increasingly fragmented and tribalistic, with different constituencies claiming that theirs is the 'right' way. These days, at many research conferences, you can hear people claim, 'My version of action research is the right one', implying that other versions are not. Consequently, the field divides further: some people accept action research as a broad, everyday form of enquiry that focuses on everyday matters ('How do I fix this car?' becomes as legitimate a research question as 'How do I learn to manage this organisation more democratically?'), whereas others accept action research only as undertaken along the narrow corridor of a project that will lead to specific outcomes.
- from without: unfairness happens when the traditionalist Academy watches developments in the field, co-opts anything that looks interesting (and is, therefore, potentially dangerous to the Academy's power) and turns it into a domesticated form that it can control. This is everywhere evident in the field of action research. Many institutions allow action enquiries only on condition that they are of the right kind. It is also

evident within higher education institutions themselves. Many academics wish to study their practices but encounter difficulties when managers who do not accept action research as a legitimate form of research refuse them permission to do so.

However, perhaps the deepest unfairness appears in how the existing system of unfairness is maintained through a process of hegemony, that is, the ability of person A to persuade person B to believe that person A is right, and to believe that this situation is person B's idea in the first place. Person B becomes both complicit in the conspiracy and also the key mover in their own subjugation. Practitioners are persuaded to believe that they cannot do high-quality research or writing, which maintains the superiority of established academic researchers.

How to combat the unfairness? Several options are available.

You can agree with authors such as Michel de Certeau (1984), who says that to enter the territories of such debates is to enter behind enemy lines. The field of academic writing could be seen as one such territory. The way to survive behind those lines, says de Certeau, is to develop tactics that will safeguard you and that will, it is hoped, eventually subvert the system by which the system maintains its power over you. To a certain extent, I agree with de Certeau, but I think influencing what counts as academic work, and academic writing in particular, calls perhaps for more subtle actions that are often best conducted under the radar. These actions involve learning how to write well, how to navigate the politics of writing in academic contexts, and how to win through on your own terms.

This is why I have written the book, to produce workable ideas that help you to say, 'I can do this too'. The book will be vindicated if it helps you to produce your report or dissertation and show that you have done it.

Now let me comment on some technical matters.

WORKING WITH THE BOOK

To get the best out of the book, you should read it in the order in which it is presented. You should also read the part pages: these set out what the coming chapters will say. Be aware, however, that this is more than a 'how to do' book on writing practices, although it contains 'how to do' elements. It goes further and presents ideas about the philosophy of writing, as well as useful models that may help you develop your own writing practices. I am always chary of models, because readers often come to think that the model is the reality, rather than a representation of a particular view of reality at a certain place and a certain time. Also, readers often think that a model is an author's final word on a topic, whereas, in my case, it is usually just the beginning. I change my thinking virtually every day about how ideas can come together. However, at some point, you have to draw a line and actually send the work to the publisher, which means that you have to put new thinking into a new text. Watch this space.

A NOTE ON TERMINOLOGY

Throughout, I use the words 'academic', to refer to the job description of a person who works in the Academy (higher education), and 'practitioner', to refer to all people, including academics, who work in workplaces, including in the Academy. The reason I hold this view is because, in earlier times, after taking early retirement from my position as deputy head teacher in a large secondary school, I purchased and ran a seaside gift shop, where I sold buckets and spades while also studying for my doctorate and writing books. I used to read and write during quiet times while sitting at the till. I currently run my own consultancy business. From experience, therefore, as well as from my own commitments to equality and the right of all human beings to be valued for who they are, I do not accept artificial distinctions between being an academic and being a practitioner. These are terms of convenience, not reflections of reality.

I see the idea of work in the broad sense of a productive form of living. You are working when you are thinking on the bus as much as when you are conducting an orchestra.

I use the word 'text' to refer to any stretch of writing, short or long. I use the words 'report' and 'dissertation', as appropriate, to refer to the text you produce as a written assignment, while recognising that the mainstream research literatures rightly see 'texts' as also referring to physical performance, such as dance or artwork. In this book, I refer to writing as the signs you make on paper or screen. Things are unfortunately complicated, because 'dissertation' in the UK refers to a master's report, whereas in the USA it refers to doctoral reports (which are called theses in the UK). There is no pleasing everyone, so I will stick with the UK convention, as the UK is where I live.

A NOTE ON THE RESEARCH BASE OF THE BOOK

All the examples in the book are taken from published work that I have supported or been involved with. They are numbered sequentially throughout the book. These works take the form of texts produced at undergraduate and postgraduate level, book chapters and books, journal articles, emails, tape-recorded conversations and other forms of writing: all are part of the extensive and rich database that shows the idea of helping others to learn how to value and develop their own learning. I hope I do them justice.

A NOTE ON MY CONTEXTS

I currently work across sectors, disciplines and continents, often in higher education contexts, where I support the doctoral enquiries of academic staff. I also work with institutions that wish to support the development of organisational research cultures. I am privileged to work with colleagues around the world, often in non-institutional settings such as in villages and townships, as well as in formal workplaces.

Finally, I hope you find the book useful. I have enjoyed writing it and working with ideas that I have been playing with for a long time. This is not the end of the story, though, because I know full well that the ideas will change tomorrow, and new writing will emerge. This is part of the enjoyment of being alive, having faith that each day, each moment, brings new opportunities for new thinking. What a privilege.

Please contact me at jeanmcniff@mac.com or on www.jeanmcniff.com. Watch this space, or better, create your own space where others can come and visit you and celebrate your amazing talent and gift for writing. You won't know what you can do until you do it.

Jean McNiff
Dorset, June 2015

Chapter 1

Prologue: what do I need to know about action research? Why do I need to know it?

This chapter acts by way of a prologue that sets the scene and provides important background information for the main story of the book. The main story is about writing up your action research project. The chapter works on the assumption that, if you want to write about action research, you first need to know what action research is, what it involves, how you do it, why you should do it, and what some of the benefits might be. The chapter is organised to cover all these points. It offers, in summarised form, the main issues from the companion book *You and Your Action Research Project*.

At a minimum, you need to know the following:

- what is involved in doing action research;
- how to do action research;
- why you should do action research, and some of the implications involved.

These issues become the content of the chapter. After this chapter, the focus changes to writing.

First, however, you need to think about the aim of doing any kind of research, including action research. Here are some ideas.

The aim of doing any kind of research is to find out something that you do not already know: research is about discovering existing knowledge or creating new knowledge. Discovering or creating knowledge enables you to claim that you know something that you did not know before: this becomes your claim to knowledge. Further, knowledge can contribute to theory; the word 'theory', broadly speaking, means 'an explanation'. You can both say what you know now and also explain and analyse how you have come to know it. Therefore, if you can explain and analyse what you have done in your practice, you can claim that you have generated a personal theory of practice.

However, if you make a claim to knowledge, you cannot expect people to believe you unless you can show how you have tested the validity, or truthfulness, of the claim. This involves producing authenticated evidence to show that what you are saying is true, and you are not just making it up. You would describe, explain and analyse what you have done, and these descriptions, explanations and analyses contribute to verification procedures; they help confer validity and legitimacy on your research and your claim, and therefore on you, the researcher.

Now consider how these ideas inform the processes of doing action research. The first question to ask is, what is involved in doing action research?

WHAT IS INVOLVED IN DOING ACTION RESEARCH?

This section considers:

- what action research is, and what it is not;
- some core principles and practices of action research;
- different approaches to action research.

What action research is, and what it is not

Here are some general ideas from the literatures about what action research is. We later go on to consider what action research is not.

What action research is

Action research is a special form of research that is located in the real world, so that it becomes a form of real-world research (Robson, 2011). It is about taking action in action for social and political action, and then explaining to others what you have done, why you have done it, and what you hope to achieve by doing it. Because it is grounded in practice, action research is also often referred to as 'practice-based research'. It is also often called 'practitioner research', because it is carried out by practitioners.

Action research contains two words – 'action' and 'research' – and these refer to different things:

- 'action' refers to what you do in your different contexts, including your personal, social, organisational and political contexts.
- 'research' refers to how you find out about what you do in your different contexts, and how you can find ways to do it better.

However, although separately the words may mean different things, in action research discourses they are always interrelated and inseparable: they weave together like threads in a tapestry. When you look at a tapestry you tend to see the whole picture, rather than the individual threads, but when you analyse what goes into the tapestry, you see the importance of making sure each thread is in its right place and is going in the right direction (Figure 1.1). Each serves its particular purpose and each derives its particular meaning from the other. Similarly, the ideas of action and research are always interdependent and reciprocal. As with all complex phenomena, the whole means more than the sum of its parts.

In real-world action research, we always do things for specific reasons and purposes, and reasons and purposes also refer to different things. Reasons explain what inspires or drives you to do something ('I have started learning Norwegian for when I go to Norway'); purposes outline your goals and what you hope to achieve ('I would like to understand others and be understood when I go to Norway'). When someone asks you, 'Why are you doing that?',

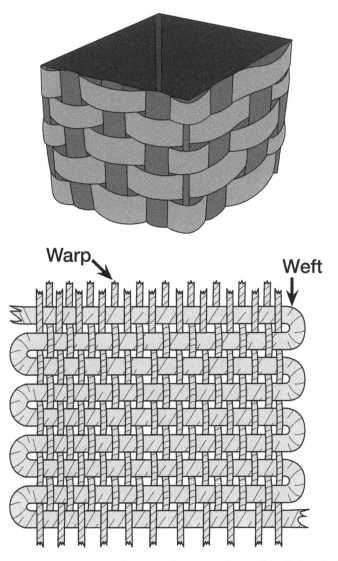

Figure 1.1 The interrelationship of parts with one another and with the whole

you state your reasons and purposes; these act as framing devices for your explanations. Further, you need to check that other people agree with what you are saying, especially when you claim that what you have done or learned has influenced personal and/or social processes of improvement.

However, these ideas of taking action, doing research and telling others what you have done can be problematic, as follows.

Taking action

There is more than one kind of action. You can take:

- unintentional action, as when you cough or trip over; this kind of action is often accidental;
- everyday action, such as watching television or doing the washing up, though these can often be undertaken with social intent and become intentional action, as in the next point;
- intentional action, as when you set out to help someone or to improve a service; this kind of action is always purposeful and undertaken to achieve specific goals; this is usually the kind of action you take in action research. (It is worth mentioning here, however, that goals may be destructive and selfish as much as beneficent and other-oriented.)

You can also have different reasons and purposes for taking action, including:

- personal action, where you act for your personal purposes: you decide to cook a meal or study for a degree;
- social action, where you act in other people's interests: you advise medical treatments or contribute to solidarity protests against injustices; this then becomes more than action: it becomes or leads into practice, when you act in a coherent and purposeful way for reasons beyond yourself;
- political action, where you act in the world to achieve certain principles and practices: you investigate institutional or corporate practices and ask questions about why things are as they are, where appropriate; this can involve risk to self and requires courage; it then becomes more than practice: it becomes praxis, that is, morally committed, purposeful practice in the world.

To summarise so far, here is what is involved in (a) doing research and (b) doing action research.

Doing research

The aim of all research is to enable you to make a knowledge claim. You can claim to have discovered existing knowledge, something that was known already, and you can also claim to have generated entirely new knowledge, something that no one knew before. However, if you are prepared to make a knowledge claim, you must test and demonstrate its validity (truthfulness, believability), to show that people can believe you. This involves producing evidence: you describe the actions you took, explain why you took them and what you hoped to achieve, gather data to show the processes involved, and produce evidence from the data in relation to identified criteria to show that what you are saying may be believed. You invite others to consider your knowledge claim and scrutinise your evidence so that they may agree (or not) that what you say is trustworthy.

Doing action research

As an action researcher, you hope that you have found new ways to improve your learning, so that you can claim that you have contributed to improving your personal and social practices and circumstances. Being able to claim this means being able to show how you have developed rigorous processes of observation (watching what is going on), reflection (thinking about whether it is good and why, and how it can be improved where necessary) and monitoring practices and gathering data (keeping records of what you and other people are doing). It has involved testing your provisional claims to knowledge (asking other people to look at your work, listen while you explain why you think it is worthwhile and give you feedback about whether you need to rethink some aspects). In this way, you have created new knowledge of your practice and you can explain the significance of your research for the new learning and growth of other people and yourself.

Now, here are some ideas about what action research is not.

What action research is not

Action research is not simply action learning or professional education, though it can involve these. Action learning is a distinctive form of learning where you learn in and from action; the focus is on learning, but not necessarily on research. Professional education is where you learn to improve your professionalism in a range of ways. Neither practice necessarily involves doing research, that is, monitoring the processes involved, gathering and analysing data from which you generate evidence to test the validity of your provisional knowledge claims, or establishing validation procedures to produce evidence that may withstand robust critique. Action research demonstrates a greater level of explanatory adequacy than action learning or professional education: you can explain how you have come to know what you know. The ideal situation, perhaps, would be to transform action learning into action research and to ensure that professional education should be evidence based.

Also, action research is not conventional social science research, which is about looking at a social situation from an outsider perspective, offering descriptions and analyses about it, and generating theories that explain what is happening. As noted earlier, the word 'theory' means, broadly speaking, 'an explanation': when you do research, you aim to describe, analyse and explain what is going on, that is, generate theory about what you see. This is what all kinds of research do, including action research, except that there is a difference in the form of theory. In conventional social science research, the form of theory is abstract: it exists in the researcher's head, in a conceptual form; these conceptual theories can help your own thinking. However, you can also generate your own theories from within your practice, in a dynamic, living form. You can say, 'I have developed my personal practical theory of dentistry practice', or, 'The validity of my theory of person-centred occupational therapy practice lies in the fact that patients say they feel more in control of their own movement'.

Example 1

Nqabisa Gungqisa writes of her experience of our master's programme in the township of Khayelitsha, South Africa. She says:

> In this programme of studies I have learned a good deal of things, sharing ideas, socializing, academic writings (my academic paper), the presentation of my findings, a boost in my self esteem and confidence, group discussions, tolerance, listening to other people's ideas, respect and other meaningful values, and my computer literacy levels have been improved.
>
> I can now make a claim that my studies have had a tremendous influence on my practice including my professional development and learning. I felt good about myself after I had made a presentation of my policy proposal and one of my colleagues on the MA in Education course gave me the following critical feedback:
>
> 'Your presentation was thought provoking . . . I was excited to realise that your epistemological values were in line with *ubuntu*. The systematic issues that informed your research should be explored more to influence practice in general and specifically for the Western Cape Education Department.'
>
> (Gungqisa, 2008: 7)

When you do social science research, you usually use what has come to be known as 'the scientific method', that is, the methods used by scientists for studying the natural world. You compare variables and say, 'If I do this, that will happen': that is, you aim to show a causal relationship. Most people in the Western intellectual tradition learn how to do this. If you wish to show that Whizzo plant food is an effective plant food for encouraging plant growth, you take a control group and an experimental group of, say, tomatoes: you feed Whizzo to the experimental group but not to the control group, and you measure the differences in outputs between the two groups. You expect the experimental group to produce bigger, better, redder and tastier tomatoes than the control group. This approach is fine for tomatoes, but not necessarily for people. Unfortunately, when social science began to be established, social scientists tended to adopt the same methods as used for the natural sciences, on the assumption that people would act in the same way as tomatoes. People, though, have minds of their own, can make their own choices and are generally unpredictable. However, the orthodox assumption remains that the form of theory generated from an assumption of 'if x, then y' will be applicable for all areas of enquiry. There is also the assumption that practitioners will apply the theories of scientists and social scientists to their practices, and this has serious consequences.

The expectation that practitioners will and should apply established theory to their practices has become normative. The word 'normative' implies both what is normal and also what should be seen as normal: it carries assumptions about the nature of what is right and who is qualified to say so. Those who generate the theory (often people in universities and boardrooms) expect those in workplaces and on shop floors to apply the theory to their practices. The main trouble is that it becomes the expectation, not only of elites, but also of practitioners themselves, who learn to accept unquestioningly what they are told and go along with what Wittgenstein (1973) called a 'language game'. In this game, people speak the lines they are given by those in positions of organisational power and do not deviate. Action research came into being in the 1930s to offer a direct challenge to this game, introducing a new game where people from all walks of life were allowed to challenge the rules and create new ones that better suited their purposes. This situation is changing, though, and another new game has entered the field called 'the politics of action research', involving the misappropriation and distortion of action research. More is said about this shortly (see also McNiff, 2013). First, consider some of the core principles of action research.

Some core principles of action research

Like all kinds of research, action research may be judged in terms of different considerations. A major consideration is methodological rigour. The advice in Box 1.1 offers a step-by-step guide to ensure that the research component of action research is of high quality.

All the contents of Box 1.1 are matters of methodological rigour; this is a major principle of action research, as well as of other kinds of research. Other principles are central to action research, too, including the following.

Action research is about practices

Practices may be conducted in different domains and professions and across sectors, in formal and informal settings. The improvement of practices in general begins with the questions, 'Why are things the way they are?

Are they satisfactory? If not, how do I/we change them?' More specifically, practitioners ask, 'How do I improve my practice?' The practices in question can be selling (McDonnell and McNiff, 2014), or nursing (McDonnell and McNiff, 2015). In this present book, the practice under investigation is writing. You study what you are doing as a writer and find ways of doing it better.

Box 1.1 Demonstrating methodological rigour

Demonstrating methodological rigour means showing that the research is systematic and coherent and addresses all aspects of methodology, as follows.

Identify a research issue

You begin any research project by identifying a research issue. In social science, the issue is set out in a tightly formulated way, usually as a hypothesis to be tested. A hypothesis takes the form of, 'If I do this, that will happen'. An action enquiry, on the other hand, begins by articulating an idea to be explored. You ask, 'I wonder what would happen if . . .', or, 'How do I learn to do this better?', or, 'How do I improve the quality of my work?' These questions are always contextualised: you give an account of the real-life social, cultural or political situations you are in.

Identify research aims and formulate a research question

All researchers state why they are doing the research (their reasons) and what they hope to achieve (their purposes). Action research questions are different from social science research questions. In social science, researchers observe a social situation from an external, out-sider position. They ask, 'What are those people doing?', and give descriptions and explanations for what they observe. Action researchers position themselves inside a social situation and ask, 'How do I understand and improve what I am doing in company with others?' The focus is on the improvement of personal learning, which involves self-reflection and a critical interrogation of personal assumptions and beliefs.

Set out a research design and draw up action plans

Designing and planning research means thinking about how to realise what you wish to achieve. You think initially about how and why you wish to conduct the research (you give a rationale) and the conceptual and practical elements involved. Action plans show how the design will be enacted and raises questions such as: 'who will be involved? How will I conduct the research? What ethical considerations are important? How will the validity of emerging knowledge claims be tested? How will I manage practical and logistical matters?' You take special care to respect ethical issues throughout.

Take action

You reflect on what needs to be done in the situation under consideration and in relation to the research question. In conventional social science research, the action is usually to conduct an experiment in which variables are manipulated to establish a cause-and-effect relationship wherever possible. In action research, the action is usually to improve learning, with a view to influencing others' and one's own thinking and behaviours and, thereby, influencing the nature of a social situation.

Gather data

All research involves observation, monitoring practice using specific data-gathering methods, and keeping records. You place the data you gather into a physical or electronic data archive. First-hand data are 'raw' data about the immediate situation, including diaries, photographs or tape-recorded conversations. Second-hand data are derivative and are contained in other people's reports or documents about the research.

Identify criteria and standards by which to make judgements about the quality of the research

Criteria and standards are involved in making judgements and may be understood as follows:

- criteria: you judge the quality of a hotel in terms of its cleanliness and warmth; the criteria for judging the quality of a hotel therefore become cleanliness and warmth: you ask, 'Is the hotel clean and warm?'
- standards: you also identify standards, which involves making value judgements about quality: you ask, 'How clean? How warm?'

You base your criteria and standards on your values. In social science research, quality is judged in terms of traditional criteria ('Are the research findings generalisable and replicable?') and traditional standards ('How well are the criteria addressed?'). In action research, your values become your criteria. Quality is judged in relation to how well you can show that you are trying to live in the direction of your values, and the extent to which you have assessed the rightness of your values against others' critical responses.

Generate evidence from the data in relation to the criteria and standards of judgement

Data and evidence are different things. 'Data' refer to the pieces of information you gather about a situation or a thing; 'evidence' refers to those pieces of data that are directly relevant to the research question and its transformation into a research claim. If you say, 'I aim to create a caring workplace where people are treated fairly and with respect', you judge the quality of workplace life in relation to the values of fairness and respect. You extract from the database those pieces that show the demonstration of fairness and respect: those pieces of data become evidence.

Make a claim to knowledge

Making a claim to knowledge means showing how knowledge has been discovered or generated, and why it should now count as valid knowledge. In action research, the claim is always related to learning in some way. The aim of the practice element of action research is to improve learning in order to improve action. The aim of the research element of action research is to show the validity of claims about how improved learning has led to improved practices.

Link the claim to existing knowledge

Research claims draw on the thinking of others in the field, whether immediate colleagues or from the literatures. Once validated, the knowledge is placed within the existing body of knowledge (all that has been written and accepted), as a valid contribution to the field.

Test the validity of the claim

When you make a claim to knowledge, you show how you have tested its validity; otherwise, your claim could be seen as your opinion or wishful thinking. In social science research, validity may be shown when other people replicate your findings by applying the same methods to their own situations. In action research, validity may be demonstrated when you show and explain how you are living your values more fully in your practice. Your values become the criteria and standards by which you make judgements about the validity of the claim and the quality of your research.

Submit the claim to critique

First, you do a personal validity check against your values to show that you are trying to live your values more fully in your practice, and you test the rightness of your values against the judgements of others. You also do a public validity check to show that you are doing this to other people's satisfaction. You also show that you are fulfilling Habermas's (1976) social and communicative criteria of comprehensibility, authenticity, truthfulness and appropriateness: you speak so that others can understand you; you show your authenticity through, say, trying to live in the direction of your values; you tell the truth such as in the production of evidence; and you demonstrate understanding of the wider contexts within which your research is located (see also page 79).

Explain the potential significance of the research and claim

You explain the significance of your research: you say how and why it is relevant, and how it gives meaning to your work and life. You show how your research may have potential for contributing to the education of yourself and other people, and for cultural and social transformation, in your own and in wider contexts.

Generate theory from the research

Different research traditions have different views about what counts as theory. Social science research sees theory as words on a page: concepts such as 'love' are explained through words only. This is a conceptual kind of theory, also called propositional theory. Action research defines practitioners' theories in terms of living practices: 'love' can be explained through the way that people act towards one another. This practice-based form of theory is embodied in the lives of real people.

Modify practice in light of the evaluation

In social science research, practitioners are expected to apply other researchers' theories to their practices. In action research, practitioners are expected to improve their own practices through learning from existing practices. They offer explanations (theories) for ongoing improvement of practice and articulate how and why their personal theories of practice should be seen as valid, usually by producing a research report.

Write a report and disseminate findings

This involves making the findings of research publicly available, in order to:

- establish the validity and, therefore, the legitimacy of the claim to knowledge;
- show how the research has been submitted to public critique;
- show how the research can potentially contribute to other people's learning, to help them improve their practices; other people, therefore, learn from and with you and can see new possibilities for their own research.

Action research is about improving learning

Conventional social science research is about problem-solving: the aim is to find final answers to problems. Action research is about problem posing, which is about asking questions. Any answers generate new questions. There is often no specific answer to real-life problems, and we just have to get along with best guesses.

Some action research texts speak about the need to plan 'an intervention'. However, interventions can often appear as interference. People don't always need others to tell them what to do, but they do need help and encouragement to find out for themselves what to do, as shown, for example, in this passage from the MA dissertation of Dot Jackson, a senior lecturer at St Mary's University, Twickenham:

> I am concerned because my students seldom challenge my role as the source of knowledge whereas I take a participative pedagogical position within the learning group to encourage shared learning. I always endeavour to move from the present situation to where we are all 'simultaneously teachers and students' (Freire 1970: 59) and recognise that in creating designs and products we are also creating knowledge. I draw on Sfard's (1998) two metaphors for learning, as requiring both the 'acquisition' of knowledge and a process of 'participation' in knowing and understanding. I am concerned about educational approaches that rely too strongly on acquiring knowledge as a collection of facts without recognising the importance of the process of participating in learning including practical experiences and reflective meta-cognition. Reflection, modification and perseverance are essential for success and young people need help in recognising their own abilities and opportunities to develop them in their own way (Land 2006).
>
> (Jackson, 2008: 10)

Action research is values-based: you try to live your values in practice

Much social science research is assumed to be values-free or values-neutral. Action research is always values-based. As an action researcher, you need to be clear about which values inspire your practices. What gives you reason to live? What gives meaning to your life? Remember that you can have nasty values as well as good ones, although ideas about what counts as 'nasty' or 'good' should always be problematised. Some people value greed and self-service, whereas others value generosity and caring for others. What makes some people think of Gandhi as a saint and Al Capone as a sinner? Both had strong family values; both believed in a strong social order. What was different about them?

Action research is collaborative and focuses on knowledge of practice

Action research is always done with others. Although you, the individual researcher, are somewhere in the middle of the enquiry, you are never alone. You always do action research *with* others, not *on* them. Doing research on others is a feature of conventional research, where others become objects of enquiry and act as data. In action research, others are always participants. Also, you are always in relation to others, historically through time and socially through practices. We are always connected with everything else.

Action research involves interrogation, deconstruction and decentring

This idea involves understanding that we are always situated: everything we do and think is part of wider social, historical and political contexts. We are born into a context with its own norms and mores, and we learn and internalise these from birth. Bourdieu (1990) speaks about the habitus, the dispositions and mindsets we acquire through living in a specific culture. Over time, we tend to accept these as the norm; we forget that we had to learn them, and that other people may not think as we do. It is essential, therefore, to interrogate how and why we come to think as we do. It is especially important when writing to remember that our discourses are informed and influenced by our histories and experiences. In Chapter 4, we consider these different kinds of discourse, and how there is no one 'grand' story: every time you try to find the source of a story, it leads you to another story.

Action research demands critical questioning

The idea that we are always historically and socially situated has implications for the kinds of questions asked in action research. It is not enough to ask, 'What is happening here?'; we must also ask, 'How is it that this is happening here?', and then, 'How do we understand what is happening here and improve it where necessary?'

Action research can contribute to social and cultural transformation

When you do action research, you deliberately set out to influence processes of change. This happens in your own thinking, where you improve your capacity for critical reflection. It also happens when trying to influence other people's thinking. Changing your thinking is a necessary condition for changing how you act. However, you cannot change other people's ways of thinking (you can, of course, do so through force or through manipulation). It is only people who can change their own thinking. You can, however, influence their thinking and inspire them also to think critically and to interrogate normative assumptions and ways of being.

Action research is a creative practice

Action research is a creative practice. Contrary to what some writers say, creativity is not a capacity that some people have and others do not have. We are all creative. Every time we say something or do something, we produce a new utterance and a new action; every line we write is a new line. As noted in the Introduction, Habermas (1975) says that we cannot not learn. Similarly, we cannot not be creative. It is essential to remember this point when writing action research.

These are some of the characteristics of action research. However, different authors have different perspectives. Consider how these are communicated through the different kinds of approach outlined in the literatures.

Different approaches to action research

Most people writing in the literatures see action research from different perspectives. Some have a broad vision, rooted in the idea of enquiry as part of everyday living, sees action research as about people learning to work together collaboratively, often for social change. Any answers you reach generate new questions that act as the starting point for a new enquiry. Others have a narrow vision of action research, used largely in institutions, where the aim is to conduct a project, often anticipating a specific conclusion.

Here is a brief overview of some of the perspectives key authors hold about action research.

Different perspectives in the literatures

Different authors comment on the history and varied traditions of action research. Most acknowledge Kurt Lewin as the originator of the term (see Lewin, 1946). Drawing on authors such as Greenwood and Levin (2007) and Herr and Anderson (2005), here are some ideas from McNiff (2014) about how different people see action research and its uses for different fields (adapted from McNiff, 2014: 21–2):

- organisational and development learning, developed sometimes as action science; see Argyris and Schön (1978) and Schön (e.g. 1983), about how organisations learn;

- participatory research: see Gaventa and Horton (1981) and Freire (1970), who use the term 'Participatory Action Research' to refer to the participation by community in the research field, now further developed by researchers such as Stringer (2007);
- participatory evaluation: this emphasises the need for the involvement of those being evaluated; see also Kushner (2000);
- the work of John Dewey (e.g. 1963) as a major influence, especially his idea of enquiry as a process of identification of problematic areas, which influenced Schön's development of 'reflecting in action' (1983) and the need for a new epistemology for a new scholarship of teaching and learning (see Boyer, 1990; Schön, 1995);
- the teacher-as-researcher movement in Britain, developed by Stenhouse in the UK (1975) and later by Elliott (1991), including at that time Carr and Kemmis (1986), who located their work within the critical theory tradition;
- the 'human inquiry' and 'cooperative inquiry' approaches of Reason, Heron, Rowan and Bradbury in the UK, and of Torbert in the US (see Reason and Rowan, 1981; Heron, 1996; Reason and Bradbury, 2001, 2008; Torbert, 2001);
- the practitioner research movement in North America, grounded in the original vision of emancipatory and collaborative action research (see Noffke, 2009);
- self-study and auto-ethnography, promoted by authors such as Bullough and Pinnegar (2004).

Many other approaches exist too, and new traditions are springing up all the time.

It is not necessary for you, at this stage of your studies, to know what all these traditions involve, though you should know that they exist. However, you do need to know this: a main point throughout is that of researcher positionality, or how the researcher positions themselves in the enquiry. You also need to decide on how you position yourself in the research and how you justify your positioning.

Researcher positionality

Different authors have different opinions about how researchers should position themselves in relation to their research and to others. Herr and Anderson (2005: 32–45) identify the following positionalities:

- insider, studying their own practices: this involves self-study, auto-biography, auto-ethnography;
- insider, working collaboratively with other insiders;
- insider, working collaboratively with outsiders;
- reciprocal collaboration between insider–outsider teams;
- outsiders, working collaboratively with insiders;

- outsiders, studying insiders;
- multiple positionalities.

Key considerations for you are as follows:

How do you see others? Do you see them as objects or as equals, as means to your ends, or as ends in themselves? Buber (1937, 2002) spoke of different kinds of relationship and how these are manifested in our discourses. According to Buber, when we engage with another, we can position them as an 'It', where they become an object in our space, or a 'Thou', where we see them as a person with whom we are in an equal and spiritual relationship. We choose whether to develop 'I–It' or 'I–Thou' relationships (see also Chapter 8 in this book). This influences how we configure the research field and raises questions such as:

- who does the research? Who makes decisions about who does the research?
- who writes the report? Who gets the credit for doing the research? Who generates the theory? Theory about what? Theory about whom?
- who decides these things? Whose voice is heard? Does everyone speak for themselves, or do some speak on behalf of others?

This is especially important if you are doing a project and then writing it up. You need to be clear about the relationships involved: the project is something you do with others, whereas the text is something you do by yourself, while drawing on the learning you developed with others. In writing your text, you have to speak for yourself and make clear how the relationship has changed from doing the project to writing the report.

Now look at how you do action research.

HOW DO YOU DO ACTION RESEARCH?

Action research is a practical, common-sense way of understanding your practice and improving it as necessary. This involves critiquing what is being said by others, as well as what you have come to believe. You begin by asking, 'What is going on here?' This can apply to what is going on in the social situation you are part of, and also to your own thinking and understanding. For example, you may ask, 'How do we find out why enrolments have decreased in our unit over the last year?'

Action research is a disciplined, systematic process where you:

- review your current practice in the specific social situation you are in;
- identify an area you wish to study and improve;
- gather data about the existing situation;
- ask questions about how you can improve it;
- try it out and take stock of what happens;
- continue to monitor progress and begin to generate evidence;

- evaluate progress and establish procedures for making judgements about what is happening;
- test the validity of emerging knowledge claims;
- modify practice in light of the evaluation;
- explain the significance of what you are doing orally or in writing.

This process tends to take the general form of a cycle of action, reflection and modified action in light of the evaluation, as in Figure 1.2.

This notional plan can be turned into a set of reflective questions, as follows:

- what issue do I wish to investigate? What is my concern?
- why do I want to investigate this area? Why is it important? Why am I concerned?
- how do I show the situation as it is? What kind of baseline data do I need to gather to do this?
- what can I do about the situation? What will I do? How will I do it?
- how will I gather data and generate evidence to show the situation as it develops?
- how do I check that any conclusions I come to are reasonably fair and justifiable? How do I test the validity of any provisional claims to knowledge?
- how do I modify my ideas and practices in light of my evaluation?
- how do I explain the significance of what I am doing?

(See also McNiff, 2013; adapted from the original Barrett and Whitehead, 1985.)

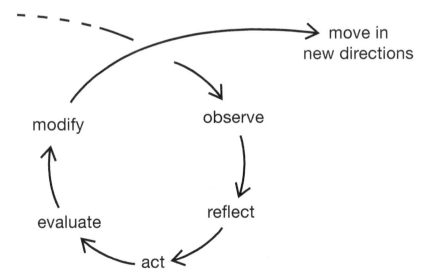

Figure 1.2 Cycle of action, reflection and modified action

In practical terms, this means that you would:

- identify a particular concern or issue that you want to find out more about;
- gather initial baseline data to show what the current situation is like and show why the situation needs investigating;
- try out a different way of doing things;
- monitor what you and others are doing on an ongoing basis and continue to collect data;
- reflect on what is happening;
- generate evidence from the data and establish its authenticity;
- check out any new understandings with others;
- develop new practices in light of your findings that may or may not be more successful than previous ones;
- be prepared to explain to others the significance of what you are doing and its potential implications for others.

A notional action plan could be like the one in Box 1.2.

The process of 'observe – reflect – act – evaluate – modify – move in new directions' is generally known as action–reflection, though no single term is used in the literature. Because the process is cyclical, it tends to be referred to as an action–reflection cycle (Figure 1.2), and because it is open-ended, dynamic and transformational it may be known as educational. The process is ongoing because, as soon as we reach a provisional point where we feel things are satisfactory, that point immediately raises new questions, and it is time to begin again. Visual models may be found in Elliott (1991) and others. In 1984, I outlined my idea that action research processes can never be seen as one-dimensional, because issues may generate other issues, which may need to be dealt with before it is possible to proceed with the main issue. I produced the model in Figure 1.3 to communicate this generative and unpredictable aspect of action research, and this model has been adapted and further developed in several places. The implications of these ideas are explored below.

Now consider why you should do action research and some of the implications.

WHY YOU SHOULD DO ACTION RESEARCH: POLITICS AND PRACTICES

This section offers ideas about why you should do action research. I organise the ideas as suggested by Susan Noffke (2009), who spoke about the professional, personal and political dimensions of action research, 'the multiple layers of assumptions, purposes and practices' (page 8), and by Sharples (1999), who speaks about writing 'In the head, on the page, for the world'. However, I change the order into the personal, professional and political: for

Box 1.2 Building local competence, supporting local amputees

This is a true story of colleagues from Norway who work in war-ravaged areas, including Iraq, Iran, Afghanistan, Angola, Vietnam and Cambodia. I am privileged to work with them to find ways of evaluating and disseminating their work and showing the value of helping people to help themselves. The people in question are Hans Husum, Margit Steinholt and Odd Edvardsen. This story is located in Cambodia.

Identify a particular concern or issue that you want to find out more about

The specific area in Cambodia – Battambang Province – has an exceptionally high incidence of amputees, because of landmine injuries, especially among the rural male farmers who work in the fields where many landmines have been left behind after the wars in those regions. The team from Norway worked initially with local people to address issues of the mortality rate and then turned their attention to the prosthesis situation. The 'official' prostheses supplied by the Red Cross were not meeting the needs of the local amputees: for example, they were unsuitable for people working on rough ground and wore out quickly. Replacements could be obtained only by travelling to a distant town. This had implications for cost and missed work time.

Gather initial data to show what the initial situation is like and show why the situation needs investigating

The team set up working groups with local people so that collaborative teams emerged to look at the current situation and find ways of dealing with the difficulties. These teams gathered data through interviewing local people and making films of people walking about and demonstrating the difficulties of using the existing prostheses.

Try out a different way of doing things

They decided to investigate, with the locals, the possibility of making their own prostheses. They engaged a prosthesis technician with experience from other war zones, Björn Karlsson, to develop options using cheap local materials to construct locally made prostheses. They used materials such as water pipes and made the prostheses sturdier and more appropriate for the local conditions. This meant that they could supply more people, and the cost was much lower.

Monitor what you and others are doing on an ongoing basis: reflect on what is happening

The team comprising the Norwegian group, the local people and users of prostheses constantly monitored feedback and discussion. They considered suggestions for changes from users to ensure that their needs were being met. These changes were then tried and modified to give incremental improvements. The actual use of prostheses, mostly legs, also became data to show how successful they were and any problems arising. At the same time that they were developing these materials, they were also training local people, to help them learn how to do this independently.

Generate evidence from the data and establish its authenticity

Interview and film evidence became a regular record of problems, issues, improvements and progress. Over time, more local people became confident enough to come forward, make suggestions and join in the groups. Their stories of their experiences were valuable to the development of the prostheses. The team compiled a strong evidence base from the data, comprising films, tape-recorded interviews and written accounts to show that the quality of life for amputees, families and the community had improved significantly, and that they felt more in control of their own futures.

Check out new understandings with others

Because there was an ongoing dialogue, understandings were negotiated and agreed on an everyday basis. In this way, knowledge was constructed collaboratively between the different members of the group, including the locals and visitors.

Develop new practices in light of your findings

This initially experimental development work led to the establishment of a local limb-fitting centre. It is significant that this area has the highest incidence of amputees in the world. The centre today is staffed and run by amputees who have been trained in measuring, manufacturing and fitting prostheses. This has also given employment to local people, improved communications and avoided the need to travel to far-away towns for any adjustments to the prostheses.

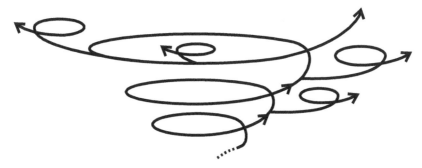

Figure 1.3 Visual to represent a generative transformational evolutionary system
Source: McNiff, 1984

me, all understanding, knowledge and decisions about practices begin with the individual, who is always in relation with others and can, therefore, potentially influence their thinking. Hence, individual influence can influence the personal and professional learning of others, which in turn can influence political processes. The personal, professional and political may also be expressed as 'for you', 'for others' and 'for the world'. It is always the case that action research is not done only for oneself, because its philosophy is premised on the idea that the individual is always in relation with and for other people. We never act unilaterally. Even when we think we do, we do so within the always already social–historical–cultural context in which we are situated. We can never get away from this.

Doing action research for yourself

When you do action research for yourself, you do so with specific aims, including the following.

We are all regularly bombarded with information, much of which is informed by research of some kind. In this sense, we are all consumers of research. It is, then, important to do research ourselves into the information we are receiving, to check whether it is authentic and credible. In this way, we develop our critical capacity in order to test the validity of what we hear and choose to believe.

Through doing research, however, we also develop our capacity to produce research. We recognise that we are situated in a specific situation in our world and we investigate that world in order to understand it better, prior to taking action of different kinds within it. We can also contribute to the subject knowledge base of our own profession through explaining how we have improved our professional knowledge and are using it for the benefit of those we serve.

Appadurai (1996) says we have a right to research, to know what is happening in everyday situations in order to make judgements about its rightness and potential value. However, in my view, if we wish to make value judgements, it means that we also have a responsibility to research so that we make wise and thoughtful judgements and offer balanced responses to developing situations.

Above all, you demonstrate faith in your personal knowledge, the idea that you are able to contribute to public discourses about matters of import from the basis of your own knowledge of practice.

Doing action research for others

Doing research for others has several dimensions, including social and professional dimensions.

The social

The idea that practitioners can research their practices has implications for how knowledge of practice may be understood. On the one hand, it may be seen as personal knowledge that helps the individual develop insights into practices (as above), and it can also be seen as transferable knowledge that people can learn and benefit from and use in their own practices. This is not a case of applying one person's knowledge to another person's practice; it is more that people can share and collaboratively develop their knowledge, which can lead to new levels of practice and knowledge mobilisation. Further, the knowledge generated by individuals and collectives can come to stand as their personal, practical theories of practice: an individual's learning can influence processes of organisational development when others in the organisation see the benefit of new ideas for their own work.

The idea that action research is always conducted collaboratively and for the benefit of others who are the 'users' of the research findings is supported by new developments in the literatures of work-based learning. In 1994, Gibbons *et al.* made a distinction between 'Mode 1' and 'Mode 2' forms of knowledge and knowledge production. Mode 1 forms are the traditional, abstract conceptual forms of knowledge: the production of this kind of knowledge requires established, one-dimensional ways of knowing, where things are seen as following one another in a set sequence, and where the aim is to contribute to established propositional theory. Mode 2 forms of knowledge are those created among people and require collaborative and exploratory ways of knowing, recognising that knowledge will develop in unexpected and diverse ways. These ways of knowing are especially relevant for work-based learning, and especially in contemporary contexts that demand working with uncertainty and ambiguity within an ever-shifting cultural and political context (see, for example, Mowles, 2015).

The professional

This idea that individuals and collectives can generate new, practical theories of practice has significant implications for professional domains, especially in relation to the question raised in the Introduction about who is qualified to do action research and, thereby, be recognised as a legitimate researcher. Two stories exemplify this point.

The first story comes from Donald Schön (1983, 1995), about the topology of professional landscapes. He said that on this landscape is a high, hard ground, populated by people who are seen as intellectual elites. Their job is to produce 'pure' theory. Down below, in the swampy lowlands (Schön's words 1983: 43, 1995: 28), live practitioners whose job is to apply the elites' pure theory to their practices. The kind of knowledge that practitioners produce is useful, everyday knowledge. The irony for Schön is that the pure theory generated by the elites often has limited use value, and yet is valued by elites and practitioners alike as legitimate theory, whereas the everyday knowledge generated by the practitioners has wide applicability, and yet may not be called valid theory. This understanding is also accepted, unquestioningly, by all.

A similar point is made in Chomsky's (2002) *Pirates and Emperors*, the title of which comes from St Augustine's *City of God*. St Augustine tells the story of a pirate captured by Alexander the Great, who asked him how he dared molest the sea. The pirate's response was to ask Alexander how he dared molest the world. He said: 'because I do it with a little ship only I am called a thief; you, doing it with a great navy, are called an Emperor' (Chomsky, 2002: vii). Similarly, when elites come up with ideas, the ideas are called theory; when practitioners come up with ideas, they are called useful knowledge. The situation extends to writing. It is assumed that only experts can write: they also have the monopoly on making judgements about what counts as high-quality writing.

Doing action research for the world

These ideas about improving one's own thinking and contributing to others' confidence and capacity to think for themselves are core to contributing to the well-being of the world. You can influence processes of social change, as demonstrated in the work of Zinn (2005), who speaks about a power that no government can withstand, and Crawshaw and Jackson (2010), who describe how small changes can lead to massive social change (see Chapter 2). However, in order to do this, you need to equip yourself to engage in public debates, as emphasised by Arendt, as follows.

In *On Revolution* (1990), Arendt argues that a main characteristic of a good society is the capacity of all citizens to engage in public debate about how they wish to live. She makes a distinction between freedom from domination, which refers to the extrication of self from all oppressive contexts, and freedom to participate in public affairs, which involves the right to unfettered speech and association. This kind of freedom is essential to protecting the development of pluralistic and diverse ways of living for all. This has big consequences for how public life should be managed and what forms of government will work. According to Chomsky (1991), there are two forms of democracy: one where people elect others to represent them, and another where people represent themselves. In the first, it is a common experience that elected representatives will end up representing themselves, rather than those who elected them. Therefore, if Arendt's ideas about self-government are to be implemented for sustainable effect, it follows that all people need to be capable of making sound judgements, and this can happen only if they are prepared to reflect on their actions and enlist the judgements of others on the rightness of those actions.

CONCLUSION

In this whistle-stop tour of action research, I have attempted to set out some of the methodological principles of action research and some implications for social and political contexts. Writing is a core piece of it. If you wish to challenge any form of hegemony or unjust practices, you need to speak your mind, but this also means that you need to know what you are talking about and, above all, how to write and communicate well. The rest of the book now focuses on helping you explore your capacity for writing, so that you can produce your account of practice to show that you are capable of speaking for yourself and know the procedures for getting people to listen to you. The focus of the book now shifts to learning to write so that you can successfully do so.

Summary

This chapter has outlined the main principles and practices of action research. Specifically, it has addressed questions about what is involved in doing action research, how you can do it, why you should do it, and some of the potential implications if you do. As part of these broader questions, the chapter has also considered what action research is and is not, some core principles of action research and different approaches to the field. Advice is offered on how to do action research, some core methodological matters and reasons for choosing action research as a preferred approach. The chapter represents a working overview of the field and some of its emerging dilemmas.

We now turn to Part I of the book. Part I contains Chapters 2–4. As an introduction, on pages 35–38, ideas are presented about the different ways of thinking about writing, and how this involves moving across different conceptual spaces. Chapter 2 sets things rolling by suggesting ways in which you can design a text and plan for its writing.

Part I

Designing and planning your text

This part is about designing and planning your text. Like most creative processes, writing a text involves different practices. You think about what you wish to do and imagine ways in which you could do it, try it out to see if it works and check with other people to see if you are on the right track. You reflect constantly on the process as you do it, so that you are reasonably satisfied that it hangs together and achieves what you want it to achieve. This is a straightforward action research process. Also, the practices in question may appear to be freestanding, but they are not. They work together as part of a creative process, the meaning of which emerges as you work with it.

Writing a text means producing a piece of writing that communicates what you wish to say to your reader in such a way that your reader will immediately see what you are getting at and will want to listen to you. This involves moving into different conceptual spaces at different times, where you focus on different ideas and use different thought processes. It helps you to:

- get your reader's attention;
- engage their interest;
- arouse their desire to read your text;
- prompt them into action where they decide to read your work.

This process goes by the acronym AIDA – attention, interest, desire and action – commonly used in management and sales theory, but applicable in most practices involving communication, including writing. These ideas are explained further in Chapter 4.

When you write for a reader, you work in a range of different conceptual spaces where you do the following:

1   You think about designing an artefact called a text; this involves thinking about what your text will look like and its overall shape.

Table P.1 Different conceptual spaces for different purposes

Design space: thinking about production of a text	Production space: producing content for your reader	Communications space: communicating with your reader	Analysis and synthesis space: articulating the significance of your work for your reader	Meta-reflection space: reflecting critically on the process you have gone through
Thinking about what the text will look like: thinking about content, style, form of text. You ask, 'What do I write about? Which practices do I select?' This usually happens at the design phase. You ask, 'How do I demonstrate methodological rigour? How do I move from description to explanation as I produce my text?'	Thinking about content, i.e. what goes into a text; organisation of chapters. This usually happens at the composing phase. You ask, 'How many chapters do I write? How do I organize them into sections? How many words per chapter? What sequence of chapters?'	Thinking about how to communicate: this involves thinking about form of words, writing style, length of sentences, composition of text, signposting, offering clues and dropping hints. This usually happens at the communications stage. You ask, 'How do I ensure that I am writing for a reader? What textual devices and strategies do I use to help me do so?'	Analysing and synthesising what you have done at the level of work-based practice and at the level of writing. You explain to your reader the significance of what you have done, both at the level of practice and at the level of writing.	Reflecting on what you have done and on the learning that has come out of it. You bring this learning to your next writing task.

2   You produce your text; this involves thinking about what goes into different sections, as well as about content, form and style. The production process is multilayered and involves working from description to explanation: in other words, at increasing levels of theorisation.

3   You communicate with your reader: this involves thinking about how to work with words, sentences and paragraphs and how to communicate your ideas clearly so that your reader will see what you are getting at.

4   You articulate the significance of what you have done, both at the level of work-based practice and at the level of writing, so that your reader will see why you have done what you say you have done. They will accept your text and thereby legitimise it (and you) in the public domain. This process of analysis and synthesis comes to stand as your theory of writing practice.

5   You reflect critically at a metalevel on the process and on what you have learned. You bring this learning with you to your next writing task, and the action–reflection cycle begins again at a higher level of understanding. You become a better writer through studying what writing means for you.

Design, production, communication, articulation of significance and meta-reflection themselves therefore become specific aspects of writing practice. Each involves a different space within which you do different things, as in Figure P.1, and yet all are interrelated and integrated within the text you finally produce.

Further, these are not strictly sequential processes, where one follows another over a period of time. They are generative, transformational processes, where one is embedded within and unfolds into another, as in Figure P.1. The entire process of writing becomes a holistic developmental process, where the light shines on different parts at different times, so that you can see the integrated nature of the whole.

These matters are dealt with in detail in different chapters: Chapter 2 is about design and planning, Chapter 3 is about production, and Chapter 4 is about communication and analysis. Chapters 5–7 are about the different practices involved in production, communication and analysis, and Chapters 8 and 9 contain ideas about articulating the significance of your work; this also involves critical reflection on the process at a metalevel. Chapter 10 looks to the future with suggestions about how you can contribute further to developing the field.

So, to begin: Part I is about designing and planning your text and contains Chapters 2–4:

•   Chapter 2 outlines the processes involved in thinking about your text and planning how to do it, including thinking about the feasibility of it all.

•   Chapter 3 is about considering what goes into your text and what content you should write, that is, what story you will tell.

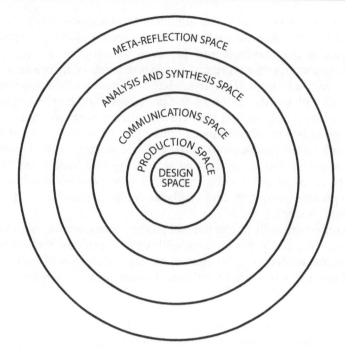

Figure P.1 Embedded and emergent processes involved in writing a text

- Chapter 4 is about communication processes and what you need to think about in order to engage your reader's attention and get them to listen to you. Bear in mind that your reader will include your academic supervisor and possibly an examiner, and they will be looking for specific things too.

Processes of designing and planning happen mainly in your head, prior to the physical writing of the text, although you can use all kinds of devices to help you work things out, such as mind maps, drawings and video memos. It is important to spend this preparatory time thinking about what producing your text will involve, so that you spend your actual writing time in purposeful ways and are confident that you are heading in the right direction.

We begin with Chapter 2, which is about designing your text and planning how you will produce it and manage the entire process.

Chapter 2

Getting ready to write: designing and planning

This chapter is about getting ready to write. Getting ready involves thinking about what you are going to write and how you will do it: in other words, what your text will look like and how you will design it. It also means imagining and planning what you need to do in order to achieve your vision. A main point made throughout is that this process of designing and planning can work most effectively when you think about it consciously as an action enquiry.

The chapter is organised as the following sections:

• designing your action research text
• planning to write: writing as action research.

DESIGNING YOUR ACTION RESEARCH TEXT

When you design something, you have a sense of what it will be like: you have a sense of the car you would like to create, or the melody, or the landscaped garden. This may not be a mental picture: it could be a felt shape or a sense of balance. A colleague once said to me, 'Writing is easy for you; you are good with words', which is actually far from reality. A text for me begins as a vague shape somewhere in the middle of my body and emerges over time as both shape and colour; later, it takes on a more solid form and moves along clearer lines into the head. It is only when I have got the sense of form right that I begin to put words to it. Also, putting the indescribable into words can be difficult. Design, I think, means enabling this initially indefinable sense of vision to emerge into the daylight as a clearly definable shape. It may be that all creative work involves a sense of design. Architects and musicians have a sense of what the end product will look or sound like, and some spend a good deal of time at the beginning of a project thinking about what is needed in terms of conceptual and practical resources to help them realise the vision.

Writers do this too. Although they may not have an exact sense of what they wish to say or how they are going to say it, they know that they have something to say, who they want to say it to, how they want to say it, and why it is important to say it. Writing then becomes a form of creative design: in the words of Herr and Anderson (2005), you design the plane while flying it. The aim of this chapter is to help you clarify what will help you realise your vision and make it explicit.

However, producing a text is more than just having a sense of vision or putting words on to paper or screen; it is also about communicating your ideas to another person. This means that, before you begin to write, you need to think about the following questions:

1   what do you want to say?
2   who do you want to say it to?
3   how are you going to say it?
4   why do you want to say it?

Responding to these questions can help you to come up with ideas that will let you shape and plan your text. Here are some ideas about how to do it.

What do you want to say?

When you write up your project, you speak in the past tense. You say, 'Let me tell you what I did'. Your text takes the form of a story: it is the story of what you did in your research, what you found out (this is your knowledge claim), why you think the findings (claim) are important, and who they may be important for.

Sometimes, people find it initially difficult to say what their knowledge claim is, but it is essential to be as clear as possible about it before you begin writing. Strategies to help you clarify what your claim is would be to ask, 'What do I know now that I did not know before?', and, 'What have I learned through doing the research?' You may have learned about substantive issues – about a topic or subject matter, such as dentistry or machine engineering – and you may also have learned about yourself and your own learning. Sometimes, these aspects go in parallel or are intertwined: you discover things about your topic through exploring how you think about it.

Here are some examples of knowledge claims:

> The writers of this book have had the pleasure of working with many student practitioners over the years and see this text as a celebration of those students' achievements. In using examples of research projects carried out in a range of settings and by students from differing backgrounds we hope to demonstrate to our readers that anyone can carry out small-scale good quality research.
>
> (Walker and Solvason, 2014: 1)

The claim I am making is that my leadership influences an effective team and that the purpose of this research is to further enquire into how I improve my leadership. However, I am aware of the need to validate this claim, preferably using evidence from several sources. This will ensure triangulation of my research.

(Barnes, 2009, as part of his master's studies in a programme delivered in Khayelitsha, South Africa)

It can help to discuss ideas with your critical friends or supervisor. Try telling them what your research is about in ten words, perhaps as a newspaper headline, or prepare a slide presentation for colleagues, where the title takes the form of your knowledge claim: for example, 'Towards a more egalitarian organisation' or 'My journey towards greater understanding of the power of indigenous knowledge'.

It can also help to write about what you have learned: the dynamic process of writing can itself help to clarify ideas by bringing them to the surface, so that you can look at them and find new meanings in the way the words move along together.

Remember also that you do not need to go looking outside yourself for a research topic, which is usually the case in social science research. In action research, you look into your own learning and your awareness of your own situatedness.

Once you are clear about what your knowledge claim is, begin to think about how you will incorporate it into your text. At this point, it may be helpful to think of the legend of Theseus and the Minotaur. When Theseus went to find the Minotaur, he had to find his way through a maze. The goddess Ariadne gave him a golden thread to tie to the gatepost and unwind as he went. He could then retrace his steps back to the gate by following the golden thread. Your text should have this golden thread running through it. It runs from the beginning of your thesis, where you set out what your knowledge claim is, to the end, where you explain how you have tested its validity (believability) and why you feel that the claim should now be legitimated. These matters are dealt with in detail in Chapter 7, where you can find ideas about how to structure your text.

Now, consider who you are writing for. This means developing a sense of audience.

Who do you want to say it to? Developing a sense of audience

In a sense, all writing begins in the head, and all writing is written for a real or imaginary reader. Even if you write a letter that you never intend to send, you still write for a reader. You may have many different readers in different spaces: you can be your own reader when you write for yourself in your personal space; you can write for others in social and organisational spaces; and you can write for policymakers and implementers in political spaces. Writing for these different audiences shows how writing can be a transformative process, where personal goals transform into social goals, with possible implications for political goals.

Developing a sense of audience also means understanding the importance of working in different conceptual spaces for different purposes. Sharples (1999), for example, speaks about writing in the head, writing with the page and writing in the world. Writing in the head refers to writing that enables you to engage with your own thinking. You write down ideas and reflections about your reading; you keep a record of learning in a journal. This tends to be private writing that draws on ideas from the literatures or your own experience, helps you to rethink existing ideas and create new knowledge, and enables you to engage creatively with your text. He then speaks about writing with the page, where you begin to organise your work environment and create, design and compose text with a reader in mind. His third category is writing in the world, where you write for social, political and cultural effect. Each of these spaces is relevant to action research, because action research also offers spaces for personal reflection, social engagement and political influence.

Look at what the processes involve.

Writing for yourself

Most of us write for ourselves at some point. In everyday, basic contexts, we write for practical reasons. We write shopping lists and to-do lists; we write memos and keep records and diaries. These all act as aides-memoires. We also keep records, such as when we gather data and generate evidence of developing practices and understanding.

Much of this kind of writing is factual and transactional, but it can also be reflective writing (Sharples's 'writing in the head'). Reflective writing helps you engage with your own thinking and use your present thinking to inform new thinking (another transformational process; see also Bolton, 2010). You write down ideas and reflections about your reading, or you keep a record of learning in a journal. This tends to be private writing that draws on your tacit knowledge, that is, the kind of knowledge that we know we have, and yet often find difficult to articulate. When you write your reflective diary, you try to make this implicit knowledge explicit. I wrote about these ideas in 1990:

> In writing I tap my tacit knowledge (Holly, 1989). I externalize my thought-at-competence through my action-at-performance. My writing becomes both the symbolic expression of thought (this is what I mean) and the critical reflection on that thought (do I really mean this?). My writing is both reflection-on-action (what I have written) and reflection-in-action (what I am writing). The very act of making external, through the process of writing, what is internal, in the process of thinking, allows me to formulate explicit theories about the practices I engage in intuitively.
>
> (McNiff, 1990: 56)

Similarly, in an interview, the author David Baldacci said:

> The only perfect place to write is in your head. Spend less time on assembling a physical place to write or superstitiously gathering the perfect pen, desk or writing hours and get your mind in the zone. Immerse yourself in the story to such an extent that that's all you want to work on wherever you happen to be. As a published author you will have far less time to hide away somewhere and write. You will find yourself writing on the road, on tour, in less than an ideal place. The frame of mind is what counts and will allow you to be incredibly productive. The rest of the stuff are just false obstacles that often give writers an excuse not to write.
>
> Baldacci, 2015

Writing for new beginnings

When you write for yourself, you write yourself into new beginnings. Even the act of preparing to write a sentence on a page means a certain amount of mental organisation and imagining what the new sentence will look like.

The idea of new beginnings is also important for life. Every moment of life is a new beginning: the present represents both the end of the past and the beginning of the future; each moment holds the past and the future latent within itself, in the same way that the acorn holds its history and the future oak tree already within itself. Arendt (1958) speaks about the idea of natality, that through our birth we bring something new to the world, and Said (1997) says that the future is shaped through our understandings of the past. 'Beginning' holds an entire methodology within itself. This is a methodology of hope. Kafka is reputed to have said that the meaning of life is that it stops; for me, the meaning of life is what you do with it before it stops.

These ideas about beginnings are important concepts for action research, which is also about new beginnings. If you are not happy with the way things are, you decide to change them and imagine new ways of being and acting. Every idea and action has potential promise. You take stock of what you are doing and try out new ideas and strategies that hold greater promise for the realisation of your values. These values are about more democratic and egalitarian ways of living. You find ways actively to transform unsatisfactory situations into new ones (see Example 2 on page 44).

Writing for others

Sharples (1999) speaks about writing with the page when we have something to say to others. This is public writing, where you write for a reader and aim to set out what you know and how you have come to know it. This kind of writing also acts as evidence of your own understanding.

Example 2

Hafthor Gudjonsson tells the story of the beginning of the action research movement in Iceland. He writes:

> Action research has a short history in Iceland, at least as a movement. Only five years ago it was non-existent. Now many teachers are doing action research in their schools. In addition, action research has become a respected research genre within the School of Education at the University of Iceland, attracting an increasing number of masters level student teachers . . . However, this blooming has its shadows and the shadows may be growing. Although action research has become a movement in Iceland . . . it is still a peripheral activity and even seen as something 'curious' . . . Research, skeptics say, is for the experts, not for teachers. Teachers should stick to their jobs.

Hafthor goes on to explain how he is trying to combat this trend. He says:

> I am driven by the need . . . most of all by the hope that undertaking such an enquiry may enable me and my colleagues to provide better conditions for action research to thrive in Iceland. If we understand better how things have developed so far we may be in a better position to make good decisions for the future.
>
> (Gudjonsson, 2011)

The others for whom you write might include the following:

- your academic supervisor;
- your assessor or examiner;
- your organisational manager;
- your workplace colleagues.

Your academic supervisor

The writing you produce for your academic supervisor usually takes the form of records of supervision, learning journals, progress reports and assignments. Your supervisor expects the following:

- Your text shows that you have developed subject knowledge. As a nursing student, you show that you understand the physiology of the liver.
- You have engaged with appropriate literatures at a substantive (subject, disciplines) level and at a methodological level. This shows that you have

learned from the work of colleagues and from the literatures, and that you can say what you have learned. You can also engage with academic debates and can present arguments for and against an idea.

- You can demonstrate knowledge of the practice and research contexts you are writing about.
- Your text shows the development of learning. Your record of learning would be especially evident in your learning journal or professional portfolio, but would also appear throughout any text you produce.
- Your text shows evidence of capacity for independent enquiry and independent thinking.
- Any conclusions you arrive at could potentially transform into a new enquiry.
- Your text shows your awareness of the significance of what you have done.
- Your text shows that you have followed academic guidelines in that:
  - you have submitted your work on time;
  - you have achieved the nominated criteria for the assignment or dissertation;
  - you can write coherently;
  - you have not exceeded word counts and have laid out your work as required;
  - you are keeping up to date with everything and are managing your study programme successfully.

Your assessor or examiner

Your assessor or examiner expects that you have done all the above and also that:

- You have produced an original work that reflects the quality of study you have committed to it.
- Your work contains the articulation of your understanding that you are making a knowledge claim, that you are demonstrating methodological rigour, that you have reflected critically on what you are doing, and that you acknowledge that you could have done things differently in light of your evaluation of your work.
- Your text reflects your most up-to-date knowledge.
- You have produced an error-free, readerly text (see Chapter 3) that is clearly set out and well structured.

Your organisational manager

If your studies are supported by your organisation – for example, if you are perhaps granted some release time for attending your course – your organisational manager will probably expect you to submit progress reports on a regular basis. They will expect to see that you have produced a good academic report, as above, as well as the following:

- Your research is achievable and realistic.
- Your research deals with an issue that is relevant and useful for the organisation. It will feed ideas back into the organisation that will contribute to organisational improvement and development. This will show that time and money spent on supporting your studies have been justified.
- Contributions from your research emphasise positive outcomes: any negative implications are balanced by how they can be addressed. Your findings point to structural or behavioural changes, and initiatives that encourage staff involvement in the delivery of results.

Your workplace colleagues

Your workplace colleagues will expect the following from you:

- They will wish to be reassured that any time and money spent by the organisation on your studies is worthwhile and justified, so that they will not feel you have been unfairly privileged. It is your responsibility to send them regular progress reports, so that they will feel they have been kept fully informed and included, before, during and after your research. They wish to be reassured that you are doing the research genuinely for others and not only for yourself.
- They will wish to see that any possible disruption your research has brought to their working lives has been worthwhile.
- They will wish to see that your research findings will bring benefit to their working lives, and that the implementation of any findings will be negotiated and not imposed.
- They will be pleased to see that any feedback they may have given to your draft reports has been taken seriously and included in your text. If you have included their responses, they will wish to see that you have identified them as participants and co-researchers and have acknowledged their contributions. Where negotiated, you have maintained confidentiality and anonymity.

All the above points are largely matters of common sense and courtesy towards others, but it is worth checking regularly that you are honouring your commitments to everyone involved in your research, to keep yourself on track (see Example 3 on page 47).

Writing with others

Often, writing for others can involve writing with others, as a form of collaborative writing. Collaborative writing is not yet widely spoken about in the literatures, although the idea of collaborative researching is everywhere accepted in practice-based forms of work and research. People working together can often be more effective than when they work in isolation, when

Example 3

David Taylor's research focused on finding ways to strengthen relationships throughout a pharmaceutical manufacturing company in Ireland. He writes about how he negotiated developments with colleagues.

> I discussed my proposal for the study with the engineering manager and he agreed to participate, provided that the craft persons agreed, and the study did not interfere with the objectives of the upskilling project. I explained my proposal to the craft representatives, and how the project would be conducted, and they were willing to co-operate provided their comments and observations remained confidential. I took care to assure all parties that ethical considerations would be strictly observed, and I produced ethics statements to this effect.
>
> (Taylor, 2000: 170–1)

all members of a group can draw on the strengths of individual members and develop their thinking to increasingly high levels. Collaborative working is a core feature of action research (see, for example, Winter, 1989; Stringer, 2007; Reason and Bradbury, 2008).

Happily, the field of writing collaboratively is also developing, especially through access to the Internet. Davis (2014: 7–9), for example, identifies the following benefits:

- Electronic tools promote collaborative writing and peer review.
- New writing technologies aid file management and tracking.
- Electronic writing skills are valued in today's workplace and academic communities.
- Every student can contribute and be engaged.
- Electronic writing is a natural companion to enquiry-based learning.

Similarly, Speedy and Wyatt (2014) identify a range of approaches to writing collaboratively, and Wyatt *et al.* (2011), drawing on ideas from Deleuze, promote the idea of collaborative writing as a method of enquiry. Through writing, they say, we come to new spaces where writing transforms into a way of being. Collaborative writing can also become a form of dialogue, as shown in Example 4 on page 48.

Writing for others is always undertaken with social intent and can take different forms, such as producing a set of instructions, writing a dissertation or writing a book. The text you produce is meant to inform in some way, perhaps to communicate subject knowledge or to inspire people to do things or to do them differently. You may wish to encourage them to take control

Example 4

Here is an example from my own pedagogical experiences.

At different times, I have worked with colleagues who have brilliant ideas and produce writing of the highest standard, but, for various reasons, have got stuck in their writing. A useful strategy we have developed is that the colleague would send me 100 words per day as an email. The text would not have to be in a specific order, and there would be no requirement to produce a well-formed text at this point. We would promise each other that they would write and I would respond on a daily basis as much as possible. The result has been that colleagues have begun to write systematically: the 100 words per day have always begun to form into a coherent text. My responses seem to add impetus to the development of the text, although I do not attempt to adopt a pedagogical role. After a week or so, coherent writing begins to emerge, and this brings new life to the writing process.

of their work, have more confidence in themselves, develop their self-image or speak with their own voice – 'write with their own pen', in the words of Nina Amble, a professor at Oslo and Akershus University College. Your aim is to help people to learn, to pass on your knowledge so that they learn how to do things for themselves.

We now turn to writing for the world and outline the importance of this element for you and your writing.

Writing for the world: writing for social and organisational influence

When you write, you have the potential for influence. You write for the world: for the dissemination of ideas, for challenging unjust practices or for other social and political reasons. This involves the idea of exercising educational influence.

When you do action research, you try to influence processes of personal, social and organisational renewal: you find ways of working with others so that you can influence their learning and find ways together to transform unsatisfactory practices and systems into new and better systems. Further, writing is central and has transformational power. Once writing goes into the public domain, it becomes accepted; if it is in print, it has an even stronger stamp of legitimacy. It contributes to the existing body of knowledge and has greater potential for wider influence.

In Habermas's terms of human interests (outlined below), you can show how you have moved from encouraging communicative competence to communicative action (see Chapter 4): you have encouraged others both to think about how they can take action and actually to engage in the action process. It is possible for everyone to get involved: Crawshaw and Jackson (2010) explain how small acts of resistance can contribute to, and transform into, popular social movements, and Zinn (2005) urges everyone to develop the critical capacity to interrogate public stories so that we come to our own conclusions about what is to be believed. This has considerable implications for you as a writer: how do you communicate what you are doing so that people can believe you and see that you have interrogated your own thinking and are trying to offer a balanced view? It is the responsibility of intellectuals, say Chomsky (1991) and Said (1994), to tell the truth and expose lies. From an action research perspective, it becomes the responsibility of action researchers to explain why they think as they do and how they have come to think in this way.

Example 5

Suleiman Al-Fugara was a teacher of children with special needs in a secondary school in Qatar. He writes his reflections on the significance of his action research project:

> I believe that this research can contribute to new discourses about what counts as inclusional practices and inclusional schools, within global debates about how inclusion for social justice may be realized at systemic levels (Booth and Aincscow, 2000). My action research moves from the aspirational to the realisable: colleagues and I are showing what a research-based school means in practice. . . . We hope these new discourses will regard the concept of educational research as nothing unusual. Through developing inclusional practices, schools can enable all students to appreciate the idea of 'additional educational support needs' as nothing to be ashamed of. In my view, all people are valuable and should be valued for who they are, not for an assigned label. I believe our school is setting new standards for good practice in inclusional education.
>
> (Al-Fugara, 2010)

Now, consider how you are going to say what you wish to say.

How are you going to say it?

As a participant on a higher education course, you are expected to produce a text appropriate for your reader and context. This will be an academic text to be read by your academic supervisor and possibly by an examiner. You need, therefore, to show that you are confident about basic academic subject matters (substantive issues), and that you also appreciate some of the theoretical issues involved in producing an academic text.

Some of the main substantive issues your readers will expect you to know are as follows:

1   ideas about different kinds of knowledge;
2   ideas about knowledge and human interests;
3   ideas about writerly and readerly texts.

Ideas about forms of knowledge

You need to show your understanding that there are different kinds of knowledge. The main kinds are 'know that', 'know how' and 'know at a personal level'.

Know-that knowledge

Know-that knowledge is to do with facts about the world, also known as propositional knowledge. You can say, 'I know that today is Friday', and you can test the validity of your knowledge claim against the empirical evidence of today's newspaper or the day and date on your smartphone. Know-that knowledge is essential for all kinds of research: you gather empirical data about what you are doing, which you analyse and interpret in order to produce findings or conclusions for your study. Sometimes, people regard propositional knowledge as the only kind of acceptable knowledge, and this practice of prioritising one form over another can get us into trouble. For example, in nursing, greater emphasis is sometimes paid to knowing about technology and how to manage it than to the practical, everyday care of patients (Benner *et al.*, 2010; McDonnell and McNiff, 2015), and this can have detrimental effects on many people's lives.

Know-how knowledge

Know-how knowledge is also called procedural knowledge and is to do with skills and competences. You can say, 'I know how to ride a bike', and you demonstrate the validity of your claim by showing that you can do it; that is by demonstration. Knowledge of skills and procedures is essential for most contexts, especially for practical aspects of work and research. Doing action research and writing it up involve the skilful manipulation of ideas, moving around pieces of text to form new text, and engaging critically with your own and other people's thinking, so that you produce a text with which other people also will engage.

Personal knowledge

The idea of personal knowledge is the same as tacit or intuitive knowledge: it is the kind of knowledge that we know we have, yet often find it difficult to articulate. Polanyi (1958) says that we know more than we can tell: we have a vast repertoire of unspoken, tacit knowledge that we draw on to help us make decisions about what to think and what to do. Sternberg and Horvath (1999) say that tacit knowledge is the basis of all professional practice. Schön (1983, 1995) speaks about tacit knowledge as the basis of 'knowing-in-action', and Benner (1984) speaks about the need to trust tacit knowledge in nursing. Personal knowledge links strongly with the idea of experiential knowledge; drawing on the work of Dewey (1963), we could say that all practice is rooted in the idea of knowledge learned through experience.

Ideas about knowledge and human interests

Habermas (1987) speaks about the links between knowledge and human interests. He says that what we know and what we value are influenced by our interests or purposes. He argues that human knowledge may be classified in terms of three broad sets of interests: the technical, practical and emancipatory. In 2002, and again in 2013, I added a relational and dialogical form of interest. Here is an outline of those different kinds of interest (McNiff 2002, 2013).

- *Technical interests* are mainly concerned with controlling the environment through the production of what Habermas calls technical rational knowledge, which enables us to take instrumental action. Values and emotions are often not recognised as part of instrumental discourses. Technical rationality is the form of knowledge beloved of institutions, including universities.
- *Practical interests* focus on understanding, meaning-making and interpretation; these form the basis of human interactions, which, says Habermas, can lead to communicative action. The aim of communicative action is to help people talk about their ideas with a view to understanding what is going on in their own contexts, and then taking action informed by the conclusions they reach.
- *Emancipatory interests* are about finding ways to free ourselves from dominating forces that control our thinking and actions. We develop the capacity to critique our current social situations and the historical forces that brought them into being. This enables us to take action to transform unsatisfactory situations into more satisfactory ones.
- *Relational interests* are about developing relationships with others that will help us to develop interpersonal, relational and inclusional forms of knowledge. These are essential for the development of the kind of society in which everyone may exercise their freedom and speak for themselves.
- *Dialogical interests* focus on finding ways to keep the conversation open through adopting attitudes and practices aimed at the flourishing of the other as much as of oneself. These include listening and demonstrating empathy, which involve developing an attitude of generosity and openness to the other and to life in general.

Ideas about writerly and readerly texts

The idea of writerly and readerly texts, developed by Barthes (1970), is important for the production of texts:

- A *writerly text* is a text written by a writer who is writing about their own ideas and from their own point of view. They write for themselves, not necessarily for a reader, so the reader has to do a good deal of interpretation and reconstructing of ideas. The text becomes a dynamic mediating space where writer and reader meet. When you write your draft text, you probably produce a writerly text: you know what you are writing about, though an external reader might not be able to make sense of it at this point.
- A *readerly text* is one that delivers a concrete meaning to the reader, who, therefore, is not required to reinterpret what the text is saying. The meaning of the text is already clear and unambiguous. A readerly text is written for a reader: they are given instructions about what to look out for, and summaries outline what they are supposed to have learned. Many textbooks, including this one, give advice in the form of 'do this, do that', though some also require the reader to use their imagination, which sometimes moves the text towards being a writerly text. As you move from draft writing to writing for a reader, especially an examiner, you work towards producing a readerly text, because your examiner will expect you to say exactly what you mean, with clear signposts to assist their reading. They will get frustrated if they are expected to work out the meaning of the text for themselves, though you can make the point that you hope to explore ideas further after your formal period of study.

These substantive and theoretical frameworks can help when you consider the next question, which is about why you want to say it.

Why do you want to say it?

Writers write because they have something to say for themselves and they want others to pay attention to them. They write for political effect. When you do action research, you aim to transform a situation, beginning with your own understanding. When you write about action research, you aim to persuade someone to listen to you and take seriously your claim that you have transformed your own understanding and are hoping to persuade them to do so too. Writing is often about persuading someone to believe something. In *Why I Write* (2004), George Orwell identified four great motives for writing. The first three were 'sheer egoism', 'aesthetic enthusiasm' and 'historical impulse'. The fourth was 'political purpose': 'Political purpose – using the word "political" in the widest possible sense. Desire to push the world in a certain direction, to alter people's idea of the kind of society they should strive after' (page 5).

You probably do the same, and this could be why you choose to do action research, which is about pushing yourself, and possibly the world, in a certain direction. You can achieve this best through writing. The book *I Write What I Like* (Biko, 1987) is a compilation of the writings of South African Steve Biko when he was active in the Black Consciousness Movement. In March 1973, he was banned from travelling, speaking in public and writing for publication. Such is the power of the written word, when you are banned from writing and from speaking your truth, especially when that truth challenges the orthodoxies of the status quo. In a later book, *We Write What We Like*, editor Chris van Wyk writes:

> Our freedom has given me the space to write about the ordinary people in the communities in which I was raised: the housewives, the washerwomen, shebeen owners, petty thieves, schoolteachers, shopkeepers and factory workers. And in writing about them I have shown them that they are not onlookers and passersby who watch as others make history.
>
> (2007: xv)

Similarly, you are not an onlooker. You also make history as you write your text. And when you write your text, you also need to appreciate that you are working in an environment, now an academic one, with its own rules, including ideas about the content and form of a text.

Example 6

In an account of their collaborative research in Kazakhstan, Colleen McLaughlin and Nazipa Ayubayeva outline the anxieties that teachers felt at the idea of doing research. They write:

> Building collaborative and supportive structures proved to be very important: collaboration was not a common feature of schools in Kazakhstan. There was a need to break the physical isolation of teachers across the subject departments and school. The competitive ethos meant that teachers feared 'rejection' and 'public embarrassment'. . . . This story of this reform programme and of the emotional aspects demonstrates how action research can be a process that supports deep change and that this deep change impacts upon how teachers see themselves, their classrooms and their practice. The emotional aspects cannot be ignored. . . . The process that the teachers and facilitators went through in this project was one of looking in the mirror, and seeing practice and ourselves in different ways.
>
> (McLaughlin and Ayubayeva, 2014: 65)

This, as noted in the Introduction, is the main purpose of this book: to help you celebrate your own talent and to ensure that you produce a text that will be recognised as of worth, even though some people may challenge what you say and how you say it. These ideas are explored throughout and especially in Chapters 3 and 4.

Now, consider how planning to write may be seen as an action enquiry in itself.

PLANNING TO WRITE: WRITING AS ACTION RESEARCH

Planning is part of the design process, but goes a step further. When you design something, you think about what it will look like; when you plan it, you begin moving into action. You imagine ways in which you can realise the design and implement ideas. Mainly, this initial planning phase involves taking stock of your current situation and imagining ways in which you can do something about anything that needs a closer look. (Note: this is different from the kind of planning outlined in Chapter 6, when you plan what goes into specific chapters of a text.)

Planning to write becomes a research activity in itself, part of your wider enquiry, as shown in Figure 1.2 on page 27. You observe what you are doing: you reflect on its effectiveness and imagine new ways of doing things, you try them out; you evaluate how well the new ideas are working; you modify your practice in light of your reflections; and you move in new directions in light of your evaluation. This process can also be seen as a form of evaluation, and this is an essential step before beginning to write.

This kind of planning involves thinking about two main things:

1 researching your capacity as a writer;
2 researching the logistics and feasibility of writing up your project.

Researching your capacity as a writer

Learning how to write means first learning what good writing involves and how you can achieve the appropriate standard. This is important when doing, for example, a skills-assessment audit as part of your course, or producing documentation for an annual or progress review. You can best do this by approaching the task as an action enquiry, where you identify what areas you are good at and where you could improve.

The first step is to identify what you need to improve: this becomes your research issue, from which you develop an action plan, as follows.

What is the issue I need to investigate?

First, take stock of your capacity as a writer to identify which aspect of your practice you need to investigate. You can do this using a range of strategies:

for example, you could do a SWOT (strengths, weaknesses, opportunities and threats) analysis, where you draw up a list of things you are good at and what might be some of the enhancers and inhibitors for the development of your writing capacity, as in Table 2.1.

Table 2.1 SWOT analysis of writing strengths and limitations

Strengths	Weaknesses	Opportunities	Threats
What aspects of writing am I already good at?	What aspects of writing do I need to improve?	I have the resources and people to help me at college	Does my current work situation allow me to spend time improving my writing skills?
What are my strengths as a learner?	Where do I feel less confident?	I am in the right culture; I am attending college with another colleague who is getting day release too	Will I be clever enough to learn how to write properly?
How willing am I to study?	Will I be willing to improve them?	I am enthusiastic for my topic and for getting a degree	Will I be able to afford my studies? Will I have the patience to study?

You could also do a self-audit of your personal and professional capabilities or writing skills through ticking appropriate boxes, as in Table 2.2.

Table 2.2 Self-audit of personal and professional capacities

	Needs a lot of improvement	Needs some improvement	Needs very little improvement
Tenacity			
Concentration			
Spelling			
Grammar			

Doing an exercise like the one in Table 2.2 can show you that you need to:

- learn how to spell more accurately;
- develop a greater sense of purpose;
- write more coherently;
- practise more regularly
- or improve any other area.

Why is this an issue?

Now, say why the situation is an issue, again perhaps using a self-audit approach, as follows.

I need to research this area because:

- being able to write is essential to giving proper feedback through reports to my work colleagues;
- I need to learn how to write essays;
- my assignment is due next Tuesday, and I don't know how to begin or end it.

How do I show the situation as it is?

This is where you need to do an audit of your skills and capacities. You could do this yourself, by drawing up a self-questionnaire or doing a SWOT analysis, as above, or you could make a tape-recorded conversation with a friend about your evaluation of your situation. This would enable you to make a realistic assessment of the situation. It will also give you initial data against which you can compare further data that you gather to assess the extent to which you are making progress. You could also send a piece of writing to critical friends and colleagues and ask for their feedback.

What can I do about it? What are my options? What will I decide to do?

You can think of a number of strategies to help you improve your writing skills and capacities. You can:

- take additional courses;
- register for tutorial support;
- do a self-development project;
- join a writers' group;
- enlist the help of colleagues to act as critical friends;
- read widely and eclectically;
- read 'how to' books on how to write.

How will I gather data to monitor what I am doing?

You can keep records of your achievement. Keep a reflective journal where you write down what you have done and what you have learned. You can also keep records of any feedback to assignments you get from supervisors and colleagues, possibly in the form of emails, comments for assignments, text messages and tape-recorded conversations. These will give you records of progress that will help you evaluate how you are getting on and flag up any areas that need additional attention. You can do simple exercises, such as count the number of errors you make before getting additional help in writing and then compare them with the number of errors you make afterwards. These are simple strategies that work and can also act as great motivators for renewed effort. They can also act as evidence when you draw up a professional portfolio to show to other people, possibly for a new job, so they will see that you take your work seriously.

Example 7

Tony Leach and Katie Simpson write about using emails in collaborative research, as follows:

> Nowadays, it is commonplace for growing numbers of people across the world to come together to create and inhabit virtual communities of social practice which operate outside the previously accepted norms of time and space. Moreover, the Internet has become a research platform for opening up new, innovative ways in which traditional approaches and methods of research can be used in synchronous (real time) and asynchronous (not real time) structured and semi-structured interviews with otherwise hard-to-reach research participants. Also noticeable is the increasing online use of unstructured/open structure interviews where researchers and participants become the co-creators of knowledge about experienced phenomena. In this paper we explore the possibilities for using email interviews in collaborative research, and the advantages and disadvantages when engaging in online asymmetrical conversation with co-researchers.
>
> (Leach and Simpson, 2011)

How will I ensure that any conclusions I come to are reasonably fair and accurate?

Make sure that any claims you make about your learning and improvement actually are true. Check with colleagues and critical friends, to see if they agree with your assessments of your own progress, or if they think you are deluding yourself.

How will I modify my thinking and practices in light of my evaluation?

Once you have overcome one area of difficulty, you could consider moving on to another. This is how learning happens: you use your present learning to inform your new learning. The process of learning itself takes the form of an action enquiry.

Now, think about how feasible it is to write up your project and whether you have all the resources you need.

Researching the logistics and feasibility of writing up your project

Ask yourself the following questions:

How feasible is it to think of writing up my project?
Do I need to pay special attention to any particular area?

Pay special attention to the following areas:

- Make time to write: this will involve negotiating home matters with family.
- Get support in learning how to write an assignment: this will involve negotiating matters with your supervisor, other course participants or the learning support services.
- Get IT support: this will involve visiting the IT department and finding out what services are available.
- Check with your boss that you can get time away from work to write up your dissertation.
- Consider any other area that is specific to your situation. Do a thorough stock-take of the feasibility of achieving your goal of a high-quality text.

Why is this important?

All these matters are important, because you need to concentrate on learning to write in order to be successful in your assignment. This will take time and effort and will inevitably have implications for other people, such as family and work colleagues. Producing a good text is also a matter of pride and a personal sense of accomplishment.

How can I show the situation as it is?

You can produce any piece of writing and indicate areas where your writing could be better. In terms of feasibility of writing up, you can produce a list of resources that can help you. For example, you might need a new computer and additional funding to attend a writers' retreat, so you need to check whether you can get them. If you cannot get additional funding you will need to decide whether to fund yourself – difficult, but worth it in the long run. What are you prepared to compromise on – a holiday or a degree?

What can I do about it? What will I do about it?

You can ask for advice from your supervisor or a student counsellor. You can talk with your boss. Talk with your partner and see if they are willing for you to take unpaid leave of absence. You could negotiate with your boss to change your working hours, so that you have greater flexibility of time.

Talk over all these options with your partner and supervisor and then come to a decision about whether or not you can continue with your studies. Get some self-help books from the local or college library and study how to manage your general situation.

How will I monitor progress and gather data on a regular basis?

Aim to keep a record of progress on a daily basis. Ask your partner and other family members to help you. Keep a list of the different strategies you try. Also keep a record of your learning from the experience in a learning journal. This will help you to see the progress you are making and give you encouragement. Keep all the nice emails that people send to remind you that other people want you to succeed and that you have a lot of support.

How will I change my thinking and my practices in light of my evaluation?

Try not to feel negative about possible outcomes and learn to look on the bright side. Tell yourself that you know that you can learn how to do this. Imagine a picture of yourself in your graduation gown receiving your award from the vice chancellor, or celebrating with your family; or perhaps in a smart new office as part of your career development. Keep these pictures in your mind and think of them when the going gets tough, as it does for everyone. Keep positive and enjoy the experience.

Summary

This chapter has looked at some of the issues involved in getting ready to write, which is about designing a text and planning how to write it. It has asked some core questions about what you wish to say, who you wish to say it to, how you are going to say it and why you wish to say it. While engaging with these questions, the chapter has also considered ideas about the different audiences who may read your text, forms of knowledge and human interests, and the differences between readerly and writerly texts. Advice is offered about how to research your writing practice as part of the wider issue of researching your work-based practices in general.

This chapter has offered ideas about how you can research your practices as a writer and some of the critical questions you need to ask yourself. The point is made throughout that you can research your writing practices in the same way as you can research any element of your practice.

In the next chapter, we consider what goes into an action research text and how you communicate with your reader. We highlight the core distinctions between telling a story and communicating with a reader, and offer practical examples of how this distinction may be understood and achieved.

Chapter 3

What goes into your text? How do you communicate with your reader?

This chapter is about deciding what goes into your text and giving an account of what you have done in your action research project. It is also about communicating with your reader so that they will see the significance of your research. Telling a story and communicating with a reader are different things and involve different capacities. The chapter helps you to see the difference and learn how to do both successfully. It is organised as the following sections:

- The difference between telling a story and communicating with a reader
- Different frames: from description to explication
- Writing for a reader: producing a readerly text

THE DIFFERENCE BETWEEN TELLING A STORY AND COMMUNICATING WITH A READER

When you give an account of what you did in your project, you tell a story. This is no ordinary story. It is a story of research-based practice: it describes what you have done, explains why you did it and reflects on its potential significance, that is, what it means for you and possibly for others. It also involves your reflections on different stages of the process and on the whole process. It is important to remember, however, that each person's text is different and is written from their particular perspective. Although there are certain expectations about what goes into a text, each text has to stand on its own feet and be judged on its own merit. You take control of your writing practices and produce a mature, authoritative text.

However, appreciating the need to produce a research-based story can be difficult. One of the difficulties these days is to combat the trend to regard action research simply as a form of professional development, rather than as a means for professional development. All too often, action research comes to be seen as professional development in itself. In the same vein, too many advisers and writers of textbooks take the view that action research is simply about improving social situations, often through providing an 'intervention'.

The writing up of such accounts then takes the form of storytelling, often quite simplistic, where the aim is to offer descriptions of what people did. You can often see this when you attend conferences and hear people talking about what they did: they say, 'I did this, I did that'. They do not demonstrate critical awareness of the need to say why they did it or to move beyond offering descriptions about practices to offering explanations for practices. They focus on the action and forget about the research.

However, the research element is what makes action research distinctive and an important method for professional education. It is the ability of practitioners to show that they are capable of explaining what they are doing that turns everyday stories into research stories. It is their capacity to generate evidence from the data, and explain the difference between data and evidence, that turns everyday practice into evidence-based practice. The challenge for you, therefore, is to make sure that your story is not simply a descriptive account of what you did, but an explanatory account of why you did what you did, and how you can explain its potential significance. It is not enough simply to 'tell your story': you also have to explain the story, and explain why you are telling it.

You also need to think about how to communicate it to your reader through writing, and this highlights the need to see the difference between telling a story and communicating a story, and the relationship between them. Consider the following:

When you prepare to tell your story, you move out of your design space and into your content space. This is a transformational process where your design is contained in, and transforms into, content. You then also need to think about how you will communicate the content, and this involves moving from the content space into a communications space. Content is then contained in, and transforms into, communication (Figure 3.1). The process is one of emergence and transformation, like the flower that emerges from a bud or an idea that transforms into speech.

Therefore, although at this point you focus on telling the story, you are also aware of the need to communicate the story in such a way that your reader will see what you are getting at. Managing this process seamlessly means being clear about the differences between telling a story and communicating a story. To help appreciate the differences, it can be useful to go back to the 1980s, when new ideas entered the literatures to do with the communicative aspects of writing.

From telling to communicating

Early theorists were Hayes and Flower (1980), who saw writing as a problem-solving process. A main strategy for them was to ask writers to describe what they were doing as they wrote; this enabled them to create a model of writing processes based on 'think aloud protocols'. Other important theorists were Bereiter and Scardamalia (1987), who similarly studied what children said they were thinking about as they were writing. This enabled Bereiter and

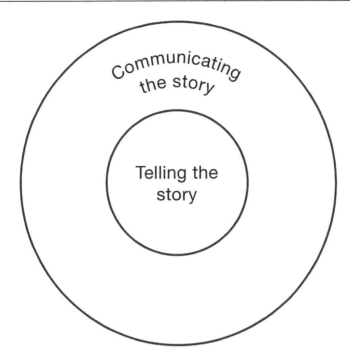

Figure 3.1 Telling is embedded within, and unfolds into, communication

Table 3.1 From knowledge telling to knowledge transforming: from story to communication

Knowledge-telling (story-telling) strategy	Knowledge-transforming (communication) strategy
I gathered data using interviews	Focus of text: data gathering and analysis Question: how do I analyse the data to communicate its importance?
I identified ten participants	How do I explain why I identified only ten? Do I need to speak about different sampling methods?

Scardamalia to distinguish between what they termed 'knowledge telling' and 'knowledge transforming' strategies. Knowledge telling, they said, is about telling the story; knowledge transforming is about communicating the story and finding ways to use the text as a means of communication, as shown in Table 3.1.

Communication is about getting your reader to recognise you, to register what you are saying and to be open to taking you seriously. It does not necessarily mean getting your reader to believe you, although this would be a bonus, but getting them at least to listen to you. It is like the idea of Iris Marion Young (2000), who spoke about a politics of recognition: getting people to talk with you begins with getting them at least to recognise you. Producing a text that communicates what you are trying to say means learning to write for a reader and considering the most effective way of communicating ideas. You can have the most excellent ideas, but if you don't know how to communicate them appropriately, the ideas themselves will be useless.

First, then, consider what is involved at the level of telling the story of practice. This itself involves working at different levels, so that you produce an explanatory research story and not simply a descriptive 'what next?' story that takes the form of 'I did this, then I did this, then I did this . . .', told as a chain of events. This would not be enough from a research perspective: you would also need to say why you did what you did and offer explanations, and this would involve reframing your initially descriptive story into ever-higher levels of explanation and analysis, as follows.

DIFFERENT FRAMES: FROM DESCRIPTION TO EXPLICATION TO ANALYSIS

An action research story does the following:

- It tells a story about what you have done in your action research. This is a research story, that is, it describes what you did – the actions you took – and why you did them. The element of explanation transforms the story from storytelling into research. The explanatory elements include saying what the issue was that you wished to investigate; why this was an issue; how you formulated a research question; how you monitored practices; how you gathered data and analysed and interpreted the data; how you came to provisional conclusions; and how you tested the validity of your emergent knowledge claims.
- This means that the story is about what you now know that you did not know before, and how you have come to know through doing the action and reflecting on your learning. It also contains your analysis of the significance of your story for your own and other people's learning. Your story is your original story and your original contribution to the literatures. No one has ever before done what you have done.
- The story explains especially how you have tried to live in the direction of your values. It also contains ideas about how you have tested the rightness of your values, thinking and practice against the ideas of other colleagues and authors.
- Stories that do the above can be seen as real-life theories of practice. You can show that you are engaging in research because you are offering theories (explanations) for what you have done and you are able to say why you have done it and what you hope to achieve.

This all means that you need to consider how you can frame your story to achieve these different elements. Each element takes the form of a different layer, as you move increasingly towards achieving explanatory adequacy. The idea of explanatory adequacy comes from Chomsky (1965), who spoke about the need for research to demonstrate observational adequacy (you show how you observed carefully and recorded what you observed); descriptive adequacy (you describe what you did); and explanatory adequacy (you are able to explain what happened). In recent work (2000), Chomsky suggests the need to go beyond explanatory adequacy, to ask: 'If this explains how things work, how do we account for why they work as they do?' These questions are at the heart of action research (we return to this point in Chapter 9).

So, how to build up these layers? Here are some ideas about how to frame your research and your research text. You will see that each layer has a new and different function and moves you to a higher level of adequacy. The layers are the following:

- descriptions, where you say what you have done;
- explanations, where you explain why you have done it (your reasons) and identified what you hoped to achieve (your purposes);
- research, where you demonstrate methodological rigour through showing how you have tested the validity and robustness of your knowledge claims;
- scholarship, where you show how you have engaged with relevant literatures;
- critical reflection, where you reflect on what you have done within your personal research context;
- dialectical reflection, where you reflect on the wider social, cultural and historical context in which your research is situated;
- meta-reflection, where you are able to stand back and look at the entire project with a dispassionate, critical eye.

To get a good sense of how this works, try doing a thought experiment. Imagine yourself to be in an open-plan shopping mall (as shown in Figure 3.2), or an airport with multiple levels and multiple stairs and escalators to take you up and down to the different levels. You can see all the upper and lower levels from every point in the building. As you write your text, you go up the escalators to achieve a higher level en route to explanatory adequacy, and to get to the top you have to achieve the lower levels. When you get to the different levels, you press a button to record the fact that you have achieved that level, though how you do this is not necessarily in sequence: you can go back down to lower levels and complete those before returning to the higher levels.

Now imagine yourself as the person on the different levels. The content in each picture is you, your 'I', and each 'I' speaks with the other 'I's. Each has a different job and their own voice, and what each has to say is equally important. They lose their strength if they speak separately: the whole in this case is desirable and would achieve a coherence that is more than the sum of its parts, but achieving this coherence is not always possible (see below).

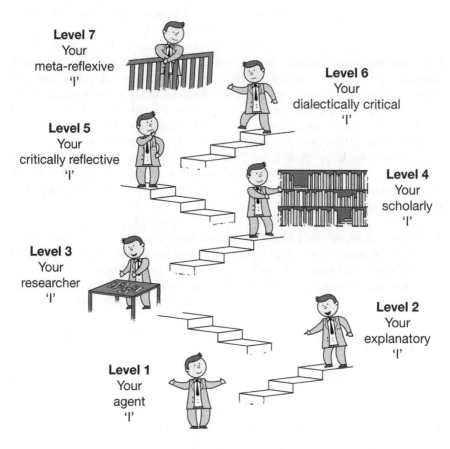

Figure 3.2 Levels of adequacy and the relationship between different 'I's in your text

The job of the different 'I's is as follows, in order of increasing theoretical adequacy:

- Level 1: Your agent 'I'. The job of your agent 'I', at a basic, ground level, is to say what they did in their workplace. Its aim was to find ways of contributing to the improvement of a particular social situation, as it asked, 'How do I improve what I am doing?' It could be that your 'I' was joined by other 'I's, in which case you would report on a collaborative action research project where the aim was to contribute to the improvement of a particular social situation as you asked, 'How do we improve what we are doing?' At the basic, ground level, you tell the story as a chain of events: you say, 'I did this, I did that; this happened, that happened'. You could go on like this until you run out of ideas or get to the end of the chain of events.

- Level 2: Your explanatory 'I'. Your explanatory 'I', on Level 2, looks down at your 'I' on Level 1 and describes and explains what they are doing. They say, 'I did this because . . .' (and gives reasons for their actions), and 'I did this in order to . . .' (and outlines their purposes).
- Level 3: Your researcher 'I'. The job of your researcher 'I' is to test the validity (truthfulness) of the emergent claims that your Level 1 'I' makes. They do this by reflecting on the quality of the action at Level 1 and the quality of the explanations at Level 2. This involves gathering data from the action and generating evidence from the data to ground the validity claim.
- Level 4: Your scholarly 'I'. On Level 4, you will find libraries and newsstands where you can read and check your own ideas against the ideas of others. Books and other texts show how other authors have dealt with the same issues that you are addressing, and you can learn a great deal from them. You can also show that you have consulted a range of literatures and that you have developed your own thinking through learning from the work of others. Your hope is, of course, that one day your work can also appear on public bookshelves.
- Level 5: Your critically reflective 'I'. Winter (1989; see also page 62) speaks about the need to interrogate your own prejudices. This becomes the job of your Level 5 'I'. It involves ideas about deconstruction and decentring. It also involves appreciating how our thinking is influenced by cultural norms and that other people may think about things differently from the way we do.
- Level 6: Your dialectically critical 'I'. Drawing again on Winter (1989), Gee (2014) and many cultural theorists, your dialectically critical 'I' is aware that we are all situated in time and space. We are always already in a context that is shaped by our cultures, histories and other economic and political forces. Whatever we think has been influenced by someone else's thinking, somewhere in space and time. Nothing comes from nowhere; everything has a beginning in our history. This means you may need to negotiate matters with other people in your current contexts, because they too have been influenced by the same forces that have influenced you.
- Level 7: Your meta-reflexive 'I'. This is where your 'I' at the top level looks down on all the others collectively and sees them for what they are: a collection of voices speaking together or against one another. This 'I' can give an analysis of the significance of the whole, or of parts of it.

It would be nice to think that all your 'I's speak in harmony, but this is seldom the case. If they did speak in harmony, you would achieve what MacIntyre (1985) calls 'narrative unity', that is, when all the pieces of your story hang together. This is somewhat idealistic. In real life, the values we espouse that inform us to act at Level 1 are not often realised at the level of critical reflection: you sometimes come to appreciate, for example, that you are saying one thing and doing another. Argyris and Schön (1995) call these different perspectives 'espoused values', which are the values we like to think we have, and 'enacted values' or 'values in use', which refers to the values we actually show in practice.

Working with these layered frameworks means that you can achieve multiple layers of increasing complexity, with each layer representing a different voice and perspective, and a different identity. You adapt your identity to your context: in a research context, you speak like a researcher; in a scholarly context, you speak like a scholar. We all have multiple identities: we are not confined to any one identity or role. As Sen (2007: xii) says, we can at any one time be, 'without any contradiction, an American citizen, of Caribbean origin, with African ancestry, a Christian, a liberal, a woman, a vegetarian, a long-distance runner, a historian', and other identities. We are not confined by labels, and we refuse labels because they are both restrictive and exclusionary.

Here are some examples to show the ideas of multiple levels of stories in action.

Examples to show the different levels of story in action

Here are some real-life stories of my work with different groups, where I encourage them to develop the capacity for critical reflection on their work.

Example 8

The first story comes from South Africa, where I was working with a group of teachers in the township of Khayelitsha on a master's programme. One of the modules was about giving a critical analysis of a paper. I asked participants to do the following tasks in small groups:

- Task 1: Take a particular event in the news. At the time, security guards had gone on strike, and one group took this as its topic.
- Task 2: They said what was happening; this produced a descriptive account. They described what the security guards were or were not doing, and reactions from the public.
- Task 3: They explained why the strike was taking place. Security guards were hoping for more pay and better conditions.
- Task 4: They considered how the situation had arisen, because of historical factors, and how media reports were influencing their own thinking.
- Task 5: They said whether or not they agreed with the security guards' action. They gave a critical commentary on, and analysis of, the situation.

- Task 6: They reflected on their own analyses and checked whether their thinking had been influenced by, perhaps, personal circumstances. Had they had good experiences with security guards? Was a member of the family a guard?
- Task 7: They reflected on the experience of doing the exercise and whether it had helped them strengthen their capacity for critique. They also considered why exercising one's critical capacity was important. The focus shifted from telling the story to analysing the need for critical analysis.

Example 9

The second story is about working with a group of six professional educators in work-based contexts on developing their capacity for writing for publication. They were all working on articles for publication and were looking for ways to organise ideas and write in a reader-friendly way.

- Task 1: We projected a piece of writing that I had prepared on to a screen so that we could make changes on the computer to appear on the screen. I had written the text so that it was deliberately wordy and poorly expressed. I also printed out the text as a document for each member of the group to work with.
- Task 2: Working in a group or in pairs when appropriate, we began to modify the text. I made the changes on the computer as colleagues suggested them. At the same time, each person had to explain to the others why they wanted to make the changes and how their proposed changes would make the text better and more publishable. This process of explaining to others was equivalent to Hayes and Flower's (1980) and Bereiter and Scardamalia's (1987) ideas about getting writers to talk about their own thinking processes as they are writing.
- Task 3: As a group and working with the original printed text, we discussed how the new text on the screen was qualitatively different from the original text and specifically in what way it was better.
- Task 4: Colleagues were invited to comment on their own process of learning through the exercise, and especially whether they felt they had enhanced their individual capacity for critique.
- Task 5: They also commented on the richness of working collaboratively and the power of co-creating knowledge about writing

practices. They commented on the importance of articulating these understandings and inviting critique from others.
- Task 6: Each colleague was invited to comment on the value of the exercise and how it had (or had not) helped them to appreciate the different elements involved in producing and critiquing a text, as well as their capacity in writing.

The strength of the exercise was later demonstrated by the fact that several members of the group successfully published their articles.

Example 10

You can see these processes at work in many places. For example, if you watch a rugby match on television, you will see the following:

First, we are taken to the commentary box, where expert commentators watch the match and report on its progress. These commentators have done a lot of preparatory work. They know, for example, the names of players, their fitness levels and likely tactics, morale, track records, strengths and weaknesses. The job of the commentators is to create an atmosphere for listeners and viewers. They do this by commenting on the weather, the crowd and the significance of the game. They give an ongoing description with some analysis. They often comment on what they think the manager or player should do. As the game unfolds, they reflect on what they are seeing. (Sometimes, when watching cricket, television viewers will turn the sound down and listen to a radio commentary to get a different point of view on the quality of the match and its potential significance.)

At half-time, we go to the studio and meet presenters who act as expert analysts. They ask questions and raise critical questions about what they are watching. This group usually contains experts in the form of retired players or possibly a currently injured player. They also usually contain a so-called non-aligned expert, such as a coach from another country. The group discusses the overall shape of the first half of the match. They describe the balance between the teams, including their strengths, power, attacking efficiency and perhaps whether one team played a more defensive game than the other. They describe the tactical changes that have taken, or might take, place. They analyse why the game followed a certain pattern, including how many points have been scored or fouls made by one side. They also explain why this is happening, comment on its significance for the game overall and the likely outcome of the match.

Now, bring yourself into the analysis. You are a knowledgeable follower of the game. You do a critical analysis of what you have seen during the match, and also of what you have heard from the commentators and analysts. You note where your interpretation is different from theirs. You are aware of the background information about the players: one plays as a back and, therefore, favours a running and passing game; another plays as a forward and so favours a strong base from which to build attacks. You are also aware that the non-aligned analyst had hoped to become the coach of one of the teams, and so may take the opportunity to criticise the current coach's strategy and tactics.

All this emphasises the fact that you need to recognise your own prejudices and your own situatedness in the event, and be more sympathetic to all sides of the argument.

Many other examples are possible, and you can see them active in everyday-life situations. Keep a note whenever you come across an example: it will help you in your writing, and especially in relation to the next point, which is about the need to write for a reader.

The next job is to communicate all this to a reader. Here are some ideas about how to do so.

WRITING FOR A READER: PRODUCING A READERLY TEXT

Possibly the most common error that most novice writers make is to write for themselves, rather than for a reader. They assume that their reader already knows what they are talking about. Most people at some point have had a conversation like this:

Did you see it?
See what?
Yesterday.
Did I see what yesterday?
You know, yesterday. You must have seen it. The game.
What game?
The match. Arsenal were great. I felt sorry for Aston Villa.
Oh you mean the football. I thought you meant the other.
What other?
The match.
What match?
The test match. You know, England New Zealand.

Oh you mean cricket.

Yes, what were you talking about? Great news about Murray, though.

It is rather like the famous comment made by Richard Nixon: 'I know you think you believe you understand what you thought I said, but I am not sure you realise that what you heard is exactly what I meant'.

When writing, it is essential not to assume that your reader already knows what you are talking about or is making sense of what you are saying. The only thing they know about you is what they read on the page. It is your responsibility to tell them what they need to know in order to understand what you are saying. This means turning your writerly text, where you use writing to work out ideas for yourself, into a readerly one, where you start thinking like your reader. You consider how you are going to communicate important ideas to them so that they can see the significance of what you are doing, as in Table 3.2, equivalent to Bereiter and Scardamalia's (1987) ideas about knowledge telling and knowledge transforming.

Table 3.2 From telling to communicating

Telling: what do I want to say?	*Communicating: how do I say it so that my reader will see what I am getting at?*
I gathered data to show the situation as it was at the beginning of my enquiry	How do I show the data? What data? Do I include statistical data at this point? How do I explain the overall situation to my reader so that they will see what I am getting at?
I involved ten participants	How do I communicate why I included only ten? How do I show my thinking regarding the selection processes I put in place? Why do I need to do this?
I identified three critical friends and also set in place a validation group	Why is it important that I tell my reader why I selected critical friends? Why do I need to explain to them the importance of setting a validation group in place?
I produced an abstract	Why is it important to include an abstract? How do I communicate the importance of this to my reader?
I outlined my findings at the end of my report and discuss the significance of what I have achieved	Why is it important to outline my findings? Will they understand what the findings are? How do I best communicate the significance of what I have achieved?

This also means building up a text using expanding frames. To illustrate how this happens, here is an example of the reports produced by children on a day's outing to Brownsea Island, accompanied by their teacher, who also produced a report.

Child's report: We got there at 10. The pathway was easy and we saw lots of them as we walked around. But we didn't stay long because of the teachers' party.

Here is the teacher's report:

This report is of a school outing, when we took the children to Brownsea Island. To get the maximum benefit we started early in the day so we were on the island by 10 a.m. We had worried that the conditions would be muddy because of the rainy weather but in fact the pathways were easily navigated. The aim of the outing was to observe migratory birds such as avocets that use the island as a stopover on their way to warmer climates. It was good to see that they were there in abundance. The children were very well behaved throughout. We could not stay as long as we would have liked because of the specially organised party to celebrate the school's centenary that had been scheduled for that evening.

The teacher's report, while obviously written in a more adult form, also gives framing information to help readers locate themselves in the story. The same principle is at work that Todorov (1990) identified. He said that different readers respond differently to a story, so it is important to recognise how a story moves from writer to reader: the author's narrative → imaginary universe evoked by the author → imaginary universe evoked by the reader → the reader's narrative (see Todorov, 1990: 42) (see Example 11, on page 74, where Jamie Oliver explains how he cooks asparagus).

What makes Jamie Oliver and others like him good at their job is their ability to speak directly to their listener and to make them want to cook asparagus. You need to cultivate the same kind of technique in telling your reader about your action research and making them want to read your report. Aim to cultivate a style like this: 'In this story I am going to tell you about my research into my practice as a dentist. It is important to tell you about it because my findings have considerable implications for future practices in dentistry . . .'

A useful strategy is to think about asking 'Wh-' questions.

Asking 'Wh-' questions

Writing for a reader means thinking like your reader. You project yourself into the shoes of your reader and ask the kinds of question your reader might ask. These include two kinds of 'Wh-' question (sometimes called heuristics), as follows:

Full 'Wh-' questions – Who? What? When? Which? Where? – give you descriptive answers. For example:

- Who did it?
- What did they say?
- When did they say it?
- Which one of them said it?
- Where did they say it?

Example 11

One of the best examples of showing the difference between telling and communicating comes from Jamie Oliver, the television cook. When he begins his demonstrations, he explains to you, his viewer, why he is doing something as he is doing it. He explains in terms of what he hopes to achieve, and why it is important. He speaks directly to you, and in such a way that it becomes part of the narrative itself. He says something like this:

> I'm going to take this little bunch of asparagus. Look at how lovely and tender these stalks are. You need to take the tender shoots so that they cook lovely and soft. It's important to get them when they are young and tender so that the taste will come out and you will enjoy them at their best.

Look at the technique he is using here. He is describing what he is doing, explaining why he is doing it and articulating the significance of his actions for your pleasure. He values cooking and he is appealing to what you value in return.

He continues:

> Take your mortar and pestle, throw in a bit of parsley, and grind it down thoroughly. This will turn the parsley into juice, and it will bring out the flavour. You can add some lemon juice if you like – here goes – to add a bit of extra tang. Then take your asparagus tips and baste them in the parsley and lemon juice – not like this [putting all the shoots in together] but like this [stroking them one at a time in the juice], because this will make sure that they are all well soaked. Now they are ready for the steamer.

He places them in the steamer, and takes them out two minutes later, saying, 'Now, look at this. Here's a meal you have cooked in next to no time, highly nutritious, and just melts in the mouth – a meal to be proud of. Mmmm'.

Semi 'Wh-' questions include How? Why?:

- How did they say it?
- Why did they say it?

Asking the first set of questions gives you descriptions of events and contexts for your study. You give your reader vital information that helps them contextualise your work and understand what the work was about, as follows:

Question	Description of action
Who did it?	I ...
What did they do?	... undertook my action enquiry ...
When did they do it?	... from 2013 to 2015 ...
Which action enquiry did they undertake?	... into my practice as a florist ...
Where did they do it?	... in a florists shop in Leeds

Asking the second set of questions gives you explanations for events, as follows:

Question	Explanation
How did they do it?	I did this on a part-time basis as part of my studies for certificated status as a florist
Why did they do it?	... so that I could improve my understanding of flower arrangement and get a good grade

You can also use the questions in a different way, as follows:

Wh- questions	'How?' and 'why?' questions
What was your research about?	Why did you do it? How did you do it?
When did you do the research? Where did you do it?	How can you best describe the contexts? How do you describe them? Why is it important to describe them?
Which participants did you involve?	Why should you include information about participants? How do you do this?
Which data do you select as evidence? Which methods do you use to analyse the data?	Why is it important to select pieces of data as evidence? How do you do this? Why should you explain which methods you use to analyse the data?

Keeping these different kinds of 'wh-' question in mind can help you to frame your text so that your reader can see what you did, why you did it, and in what way it is significant. It helps you to give descriptions and explanations, which, with refinement, can transform into your personal theories of practice (see Example 12 on page 76).

Moving from telling to communicating means moving from writing for yourself to thinking like your reader and writing for your reader. It involves moving across different head spaces, and this has implications for what goes on the page. Your readers will not appreciate the importance of what you are saying unless you tell them: it is vital to explain to them your own thinking about the importance of why you need to communicate ideas in an explicit form.

Example 12

Here is an example from the work of Tamiko Kondo, a Japanese teacher educator who is studying at York St John University. She writes:

> This account of my action research, as a Japanese doctoral candidate studying in England and working collaboratively with Japanese teachers in Japan, will be of interest to [people] who wish to learn more about Japanese curricula and policy, especially those who wish to recruit Japanese students to their institutions or to negotiate student placements in Japan. It will also show the need to critique current Japanese policies regarding the teaching and learning of English as an additional language.

Note here that she outlines what she is doing, why she is doing it, and what relevance the text will have to readers: in other words, she provides background and contextualising information about herself as author. She also draws her reader into the text and fulfils her responsibility to her reader by outlining what the text is about (its contents) and why the reader should read it (purposes).

> The Japanese government's repeated announcements of plans to reform English language education show a desire for an urgent improvement of Japanese students' English abilities; this puts considerable pressure on many Japanese English teachers. In 2013, in preparation for the 2020 Tokyo Olympic Games, the government announced the latest English education reform plan, identifying specific levels or scores in external English proficiency tests both as the goal of Japanese secondary level students and also as the requirements of English proficiency for English teachers. From a critical perspective, this instrumental approach to education and its focus on outcomes denies my values, which include a commitment towards authentic communication through the development of communicative competence, and to educationally oriented pedagogical practices.

Here, she contextualises her study in terms of its background and gives reasons why she wished to do it. Now, she moves into descriptions of actions:

> I have convened an action research group with Japanese English teachers in Japan to find ways to facilitate students' communicative competence, grow professionally, make a difference in English classrooms and cultivate a teacher research culture in Japan.
>
> (Kondo, 2015)

Further, if you can do this, you can get to the point where you are theorising your practice. This means that you can give both descriptions of, and explanations for, practice and explain the significance of what you are doing. These personal theories of practice can potentially transform into transferable theories that other people can learn from and adapt to their own practice if they wish. Understanding the need to communicate with your reader and learning how to do it will lift your report from an ordinary descriptive account into a scholarly account with explanatory potential. This is where you want to be.

Now consider: the ideas presented here refer to structural issues, that is, matters regarding the construction of texts. However, there is more: you and your reader are real human beings, located in a particular space and time, in social contexts and with social responsibilities. This means that you need to take these historical–social–cultural aspects into account, too. How to do this becomes the focus of the next chapter, which is about how to develop communicative competence.

Summary

This chapter has looked at the differences between telling a story and communicating with a reader. It has offered examples of what this looks like in action and how you can achieve both elements so that your reader also understands the differences and can put the advice given into action. A core aspect of the chapter is about how to achieve a high level of theorisation when telling stories by showing how they may be layered so that new levels of theoretical adequacy may be achieved.

Chapter 4 now moves on to considering how to develop an understanding of what counts as communicative competence and how to achieve it.

Chapter 4

Developing communicative competence: writing for a reader

Chapter 3 looked at the importance of knowing the difference between telling a story and communicating with your reader. It focused on how you tell the story of what you did in your action research. In this chapter, we now focus on what is involved in communicating, and how you can learn to do it well.

Different people think differently about what communication means or what it involves, but most agree that the aim is, broadly speaking, to transfer what is in your head into the head of another person. This means first getting the other to listen to what you are saying (your message) and then to accept it. In terms of the broader principles of action research, it is about achieving mutual understanding for social betterment.

Knowing how to speak or write so that the other person will accept what you say involves the art of rhetoric, a form of speaking or writing persuasively. In fifth-century Greece, rhetoric was a highly regarded capability, because all citizens had the right to plead their case in the open courts of justice, so the better you were at persuasion, the greater chance you had of winning a case. It is much the same when you write: the better you are at communicating, the greater the chance that your reader or listener will take your work seriously and accept what you are saying.

Many writers call this idea of knowing how to communicate 'communicative competence'. This is an important concept and includes the idea of writing for your reader. This chapter focuses on how you can develop it and is organised as the following sections:

- What does communicative competence mean? Why is it important?
- Writing for a reader, writing like a reader;
- Strategies for communicative competence: selling ideas.

In the next chapter, we look at another aspect of achieving communicative competence, which is how to read like a writer.

First, consider what the idea of communicative competence means, and why it is important.

WHAT DOES COMMUNICATIVE COMPETENCE MEAN?
WHY IS IT IMPORTANT?

The term 'communicative competence' was first coined by Noam Chomsky in 1965, as part of the study of linguistics, and specifically the study of grammar. He identified two kinds of knowledge of language: competence and performance. Competence, he said, was the speaker–hearer's internalised knowledge of language, and performance referred to the use of language in real-life situations. This abstract view was challenged by several theorists, including Hymes (1972), Widdowson (1983) and Savignon (1972, 1991), who all also saw communication as being about social interchange.

Over time, these ideas were developed across a range of disciplines, including by Habermas, who used the concept 'communicative competence' to refer to people in social situations who aim to achieve mutual under-standing (many people writing in the action research literatures, including Carr and Kemmis, base their work on Habermas's ideas: see Carr and Kemmis, 1986). One of Habermas's major contributions was to spell out what counted as communicative competence and explain how it could be judged. He set out four conditions for assessing the validity of truth claims (a truth claim is what you claim to be the case and purport to be true). Habermas said that the conditions for judging the believability of truth claims were as follows (this would refer to both speakers and writers):

- The claim should be comprehensible: the listener/reader should be able to understand what the speaker/writer is saying.
- It should be truthful: the speaker/writer should show that they are telling the truth.
- It should be authentic: the speaker/writer should show that they can be believed.
- It should be appropriate: the speaker/writer should demonstrate awareness of relevant contextualising factors (see Habermas, 1976: 2–3, for the original text).

These ideas are especially important when you focus on communication. It means that, when producing a text, you have to make sure you are writing for your reader, and this means being aware that they do not know you or your subject matter, so they need you to explain to them at every step of the way what you are saying and why they should believe you. It also involves developing what Mason (2001) calls the capacity to 'notice', which is a heightened awareness of the topic you are speaking about. John Berger (1972) also talks about this capacity: he says we should 'hold everything dear', that is, be aware of everything that is going on in the moment (see also Nixon, 2012, for an account of his work).

This can be tricky for you. How can you achieve a situation where, when writing, you are constantly aware of your reader and make sure you write for them? How do you demonstrate the validity of what you are saying in your text according to Habermas's criteria? And how do you show them that you are aware of wider issues?

Here are some of the things involved when you learn to write for your reader.

WRITING FOR A READER, WRITING LIKE A READER

Learning to write for a reader and developing communicative competence involve two sets of conditions: internal and external ones.

- Internal conditions refer to what you need to do in relation to your own thinking.
- External conditions refer to what you need to do in relation to what is going on around you.

First, look at what the internal conditions involve.

Internal conditions

These include:

- thinking of yourself as a writer;
- thinking about how you see your reader;
- developing the capacity to critique your own thinking.

Thinking of yourself as a writer

Writing for a reader means thinking of yourself as a writer. This can be difficult for some, including some adult learners returning to study, who find it hard even to think of themselves as learners and students, let alone as researchers or writers. Getting to this point involves, to a certain extent, recreating yourself. You stop thinking of yourself in terms of 'I'm an engineer' or 'I'm a plumber' and start thinking, 'I'm also a researcher' and 'I'm also a writer', so you become an engineer–researcher or a plumber–writer.

Here are some things you can do to develop this capacity.

- *Rethink ideas about creativity.* As noted earlier, some people believe that creativity is a special gift that some people have and others do not, but this is not the case. Humans are by nature creative. Every time we speak or write we say something new. It is an original work; no one has ever written it before or ever will again. Creativity is not something we have so much as what we do: we are creative rather than 'have creativity'. We are by nature creative beings.

    Some people link the idea of creativity with play, where we experiment with new forms of thinking, being and self-expression. You can develop your capacity for original thinking by using specific strategies and understandings, including the following:

- *Re-identify yourself.* This involves how you think about identity. Some people think that identity is a special something they were born with that will last for all time: they say, 'I am a "this" because I am not a "that"'. However, we all have multiple identities. A person may be at any one time a golfer, a human rights activist, an Arsenal supporter, a gardener, an Elvis fan and many other characteristics (see also Sen, 2007 on page 68), and these characteristics usually change over time and according to the persons we are with. Most of us behave differently towards someone in authority to the way we do towards a child. The issue of identity is complex and cannot be reduced to a single perspective, and it is possible consciously to change one's identity and self-perception.

  Deciding to see yourself as a writer means calling up the passion about ideas and letting it shine through your writing. Believe in your ideas and in yourself: your reader will quickly pick up whether you are passionate or are faking it.

- *Create a life.* Sennett (2009) says that we create our lives: we are our own makers. Sadly, this may not always be the case: millions of people who are trapped in difficult political situations or unhappy relationships do not have choices about how they create their lives. However, you can, at least to a certain extent, control the way you respond to life circumstances: this is your choice and frequently under your control. It is up to you how you respond to others and how you behave (see Example 13 on page 82).

- *Create a text.* When you write, you create a text. Many people use writing to work out ideas, finding ways of externalising in explicit form what is internal in the head. Writing also involves dedicated thinking time. Lisbeth Salander, in Stieg Larsson's *Millennium* trilogy (Larsson, 2008), sits near her window and thinks. Setting aside thinking time is essential: you need to sort out ideas and organise them mentally in order to write coherently. Sometimes, an idea can be elusive, so you just have to stick with it and trust in your intuition until it comes right. Always trust your instinct.

- *Develop a growth mindset.* Learn to develop a mindset where you quickly come up with original ideas. This means being open to new ideas at all times. Dweck (2006) identifies two mindsets: (1) a 'fixed mindset' that 'creates an urgency to prove yourself over and over' (page 6), and (2) a growth mindset that believes 'that a person's true potential is unknown (and unknowable); that it's impossible to foresee what can be accomplished with years of passion, toil, and training' (page 7). This is the kind of mindset needed in writing (and in action research), where you hold out the possibility that everything is possible. Your job then is to try to make it happen. It involves believing you can do it, believing you can come up with original ideas, and being on the lookout for when they arrive. Rowlands (2005) says that everything he knows he learned from TV. You can do the same. Look for links between themes across storylines.

Example 13

Here is an example of one person's reflections on how she has controlled the way she responded to life circumstances. I was involved for 3 years on a part-time professional education course for teachers in Qatar. One of the participants, Shaikha Hamad Al-Hajri, writes about how she has developed her critical capacity in appreciating the significance of her work.

My critical reflection on the significance of my action research

I have learned much from doing my action research. My evidence tells me I am justified in claiming that I have improved my practice as a presenter. My peers corroborated this claim during a later presentation at [a] workshop. All agreed that I had improved my skills and knowledge. Here are the most important things I have learned.

I have learned the value of professional patience and courage. I call this 'long patience': it sustains you during periods of lifelong learning. Being a mother of four children and a working lady, I have learned another kind of patience – 'beautiful patience' – when you live with the hope that things will be better if you remain committed to what you believe in.

I have learned the importance of meeting the other person in their own space. I have to earn their trust for them to allow me to learn from them, and for me to be part of their learning, so that they may come to accept me as a resource for learning.

I have learned the importance of values, and not to underestimate the capabilities of others and myself. . . . I wish to use this gift. I believe I am contributing to the creation of cultures of educational enquiry. There may still be far to go, but we are on the road together, each will help the other, and none will turn back.

Al-Hajri, 2015

Let your imagination run free and keep your notebook or smartphone handy to record ideas for, say, an article or assignment. Add to them as the ideas develop.

- *Draw on your tacit knowledge.* When you are focused, you think at the level of high consciousness. When you go off-focus, you open your mind to your tacit knowledge. You then work to transform your deep-level knowledge into explicit knowledge. Also remember that you cannot force this: if you think about what you are doing when you are typing, you tend to make mistakes. It is by engaging peripheral thinking that the co-ordination between head and hand happens seamlessly.

* *Be kind to yourself.* You are kind to other people, so be kind to yourself too. You are not in a competition; you don't have to prove anything (unless, of course, you have to hand in an assignment next week). Accept that you will have good days and not so good days. On less-productive days, read or think or talk with others. Be patient with yourself: you are in for the long haul, so pace yourself and take it as it comes. But don't use a slack day as an excuse not to write. Be determined and pick up with renewed energy the next day.

Now, consider the second thing you need to do when writing for a reader. This involves thinking about how you see your reader and how you position them, which is also about the ethics of writing.

* ***Think about how you see your reader.*** This idea relates to the ideas in Chapter 2 about who are you writing for. What kind of relationship do you develop between your reader and yourself? Several writers speak about these things. Buber (1937) (see also page 26), for example, says that we sometimes see others in terms of an 'It' or a 'Thou': we can develop 'I–It' and 'I–Thou' relationships (in the original German, the familiar term for 'you' is '*Du*', hence, 'Thou'). When we see a person as 'Thou', we see them in close relation. When we see them as an 'It', we see them as objects in our space, and often treat them as means to an end. The kind of thinking needed in 'I–Thou' relationships tends to be relational thinking, where we see connections between things, whereas the kind of thinking that leads us to think in terms of 'I–It' relationships tends to be an abstract, technical rational form of functionalist thinking (see also the ideas of Eikeland (2006) about 'condescending ethics', in Chapter 8) (see also Example 14 on page 84).

  So, how do you position your reader? Do you speak with them as an equal, or talk up or down to them? Do you accept that they may not agree with what you are saying, and speak in a way that respects this? Recognising that others may think differently from you refers to what is called 'theory of mind'. If you accept this, you need to communicate to your reader that, although you are reasonably confident about your own ideas, you still appreciate that they may think differently. You also recognise that you may be mistaken. (This is also one of the reasons why it is important to do a big or several small literature reviews – see Chapter 5 – where you test your ideas against other people's, and possibly change your opinions in light of their arguments.)

  To be able to do this, however, you need to develop the capacity for self-reflection and self-critique: this becomes the next internal condition for writing for a reader.

* ***Develop the capacity for self-reflection and self-critique.*** In Lewis Carroll's (1872/1994) *Through the Looking Glass*, Alice climbs through a

Example 14

In a presentation at the 2015 Value and Virtue in Practice-Based Research conference, Steve Mee, Alison Buckley and Louise Corless spoke about the following:

> We three nursing lecturer colleagues, from mental health, learning disability (proper) and adult nursing, at the University of Cumbria have attempted to make the narratives of experts by experience central to learning on the course. The experts by experience have included people with mental ill health, with a learning disability and those who have survived life-threatening illness. The nature of the learning and the breadth of impact have led the three of us to reflect on the meaning of professional education in Higher Education. All three lecturers have engaged in research in working with experts by experience.
>
> The impact has been significant in four areas:
>
> 1   On us as lecturers: the profound things we have learned from our expert by experience colleagues. What is our role as facilitators of learning?
> 2   On our students who describe nuanced and transformational learning.
> 3   In practice: what students have done differently when they go back to practice. We have collectively carried out research in this area.
> 4   On the university: the award of a teaching fellowship to a woman with a learning disability for her outstanding contribution to teaching and learning. The vice chancellor suggested that work such as this should define what the University stands for.
>
> (Mee *et al.*, 2015)

looking glass and finds herself in a world in reverse. To read text, she has to hold it up to the reverse side of the mirror so that it is the right way round. She is in some doubt now about what is 'right' or 'real'.

You also need to develop the capacity to climb through the mirror, look back at the world from a different angle and begin to question what is right, true and valuable. You need to ask, 'Do I show that I critique normative assumptions, including my own? Have I interrogated my assumptions? Do I demonstrate cultural and social sensitivity?' Foucault (1999) speaks about 'making the familiar strange', which means seeing the familiar through different eyes and reading it as a more critical version of an existing story. Bolton (2010) also develops these themes: she draws a distinction between self-reflection and reflexivity. Self-reflection, she says, involves:

an in-depth consideration of events or situations: the people involved, what they experienced, and how they felt about it. This involves reviewing or reliving the experience to bring it into focus, and replaying from diverse points of view. Seemingly innocent details might prove to be key; seemingly vital details may be irrelevant.

(Bolton, 2010: xix)

'Reflexivity' means finding a way of:

standing outside the self to examine, for example, how seemingly we are involved in creating social or professional structures counter to our espoused values. It requires being able to stay with personal uncertainty, critically informed curiosity, and flexibility to find ways of changing deeply held ways of being: a complex, highly responsible social and political activity.

(Bolton, 2010: xix)

To summarise so far, these have been some of the internal considerations necessary for learning to write for your reader. Now look at some of the external conditions necessary for developing communicative competence.

External conditions

There are many external conditions, but two of the most important are:

- understanding the self-embedded nature of story;
- engaging with the politics of writing (the new literacies).

Before going into the main text, however, here is an excerpt from the transcript of a conversation with Noam Chomsky about teaching, held in 1995.

Noam: Teaching [at primary level] ought to be very similar to graduate teaching in the sciences. Teachers might put different questions at different levels but it is not about pouring knowledge into children's ears like filling a bowl of water. Children have to explore. If they are going to learn anything it's going to be by their own exploration. In the course of that they are also going to challenge. If they are not convinced by what the teacher says they should have the right and the confidence to pursue their own convictions. As far as I can see that should happen at all levels.

Jean: It should but it doesn't.

Noam: It doesn't but it can.

Please keep this conversation in mind.

Understanding the self-embedded nature of story

Loy (2010) says that the world is made of stories: we learn them from birth as part of our cultural heritage. We mediate the stories we hear 'out there' through what we have already come to believe 'in here'. If I have internalised a story that all people have two legs, I will find it unusual when I see someone with only one: they represent a new story that is not part of my usual repertoire. Many of us tend not to be aware that we use existing stories to interpret new stories, possibly because we have learned a 'Bigger Story' that says this is the way things are and this is how they should be. 'We do not see our stories as stories because we see *through* them', says Loy, 'the world we experience as reality is constructed with them' (page vii; emphasis in original). Ely *et al.* (1997: 63) say that we are in story: story surrounds us. The difficulty is to appreciate that we live by internalised stories and need to see them for what they are (but saying this is a story too).

This idea is illustrated by a story in Loy (2010: 4):

> According to a Hindu myth, the world is upheld by the great elephant Maha Pudma, who is in turn supported by the great tortoise Chukwa.
> An Englishman asked a Hindu sage what the great tortoise rests upon.
> 'Another turtle', was the reply.
> And what supports that turtle?
> 'Ah, Sahib, after that it's turtles all the way down.'

Every story we tell is underpinned by other stories.

Example 15

Here is an example of how we internalise stories and come to believe them.

> A few years back I was with a companion in the town of Hot Springs, Arkansas. The day was wet and windy so we decided to stay close and have a look at the town. We knew that the town was famous for its gangster history and wanted to see it; many famous gangsters had visited or lived there and developed businesses, including Owney Madden (of good Irish heritage) who created the Cotton Club. We made our way to the Gangster Museum, and saw within the museum shop a lady who turned out to be Deirde Capone, grandniece of Al Capone. She was selling her book *Uncle Al Capone* (Capone, 2011), and so of course we purchased a copy, signed by her. The book tells how Uncle Al, a much-maligned figure who held strong family values and ran a legitimate business, was a man of strong character, much loved and admired. A photo on p. 167 shows three men, dressed up as cowboys, including Al, who is holding a pistol to another man's head.

All three appear to be having a good laugh. The caption, written by Deidre reads: 'This is the only photograph in existence where Al Capone has a pistol in his hand. On the back of the picture my grandmother wrote "Al plays cops & robbers while hiding out in Wisconsin. 1925"'.

(Capone, 2011: 167)

This story is different from other stories, including those of Kobler (1992) and Helmer and Bilek (2004), which outline the kinds of violent law-breaking activity that Al Capone became famous for. Which story do we believe? Do we have to believe one or the other? (That's a story.) Or can we believe both? (That's a story, too.)

We hear conflicting stories through the culture and are led to believe one or the other through various means, including a Big Story that says that we need to choose between conflicting stories, paralleled by another Big Story that says we do not. Perhaps we never find an ultimate story: perhaps there is no overarching story that tells us which stories to believe. We have to decide for ourselves and we must take full responsibility for what we choose to believe.

When you do action research, this becomes a core principle. You become critical and interrogate what you are told: things do not have to be the way they are. We can develop new stories 'in here' to change old ones, both 'in here' and 'out there'. But this can be difficult, because it means engaging in a process of reframing (Schön and Rein, 1994): that is, changing the way we see things through engaging with our own thinking.

However, some people like to believe in only one story: this then becomes what Lyotard (1984) calls a Grand Narrative, but this Grand Narrative does not recognise that there are 'local narratives'. One of the biggest institutions responsible for doing this, and for perpetuating the system where the idea of a Grand Narrative is seen as legitimate, is higher education, especially in relation to what counts as writing for publication. This means engaging with the politics of writing, and this involves what is now called 'the new literacies'.

Engaging with the politics of writing (the new literacies)

It is recognised everywhere, especially in higher education, that publication is the most powerful means of perpetuating a culture. The printed word is all-powerful. Because higher education wishes to perpetuate and reproduce itself, it insists on the legitimacy of its own stories. These are that only certain ways of thinking and writing – factual, objective, dispassionate, written in the third person and usually in the passive voice – are acceptable. The form of structure must be strictly sequential and tightly organised into established headings with specific content. Evidence is drawn mainly from statistical data through statistical analysis. Early chapters or parts of a text need to be perfected before you move on to later ones. Only those stories that conform to the rules get accepted.

Mathien and Wright, writing about philosophical writing, describe this situation as follows:

> Contemporary philosophical writing is largely impersonal and technical in style. It proposes definitions, makes arguments, criticizes other arguments, corrects previous infelicities and imprecisions in a position, and situates it all in a context of issues current in the disciplines. The canons of style are less rigid than those used in the natural sciences, and they avoid the historian's phobic avoidance of the first person singular, but they are, nevertheless, unmistakably academic and 'professional'.
>
> (2006: 1)

This is bad news for process forms of action and writing, where ideas emerge through the practice of writing itself, so that texts change as you write them. It is often not possible to produce early chapters in a final form until you have written an entire first draft. The problem for action researchers then is to fit the evolutionary form of writing into the expectations of the dominant rigid form.

Further, this insistence on so-called 'academic' forms of writing really is silly, because ideas about the legitimacy of innovative forms of writing are everywhere in the literatures. Lyotard (1984) says that the era of Grand Narratives is past. He argues instead for small, local narratives, where each person or school of thought may represent itself according to its preferred values and traditions. Ideas like this have inspired writers such as Lankshear and Knobel (2011) and Cope and Kalantzis (2000) to develop new fields such as the new literacies and multiliteracies. The messages are that it is not enough just to be literate and be able to read and write: you also have to be socially and politically literate and understand the hidden stories that inform institutional and social systems.

In real-life terms, systems that are past their sell-by date should be changed. We live in an interconnected world of intricate human interchange (Chesbrough, 2006) that recognises the need to talk with others and learn in a networked way (see Cope and Kalantzis, 2000). Collins (2010) demands, 'Bring on the books for everybody'; Sharples and van der Geest (1996) and Brown and Duguid (2000) argue that new technologies have produced a new writing environment where people learn and write together; see also Andrews and England (2012) on new digital dissertations and theses. Single-focused, one-dimensional forms are no longer relevant and, in many cases, can be damaging (see also Graff's comments (2003), as mentioned in the Introduction to this book).

So, how can the situation be changed? First, it means appreciating that, according to Habermas (1975), once a system is put in place, it becomes so taken for granted that it assumes a life of its own, often detached from real life. However, he says, if systems are created by people, they can be recreated and made to serve the needs of the people who created them. Doing this requires an eye to the future, political will and a good deal of determination. You need to exercise these qualities.

Here are some ideas about how you can do this.

STRATEGIES FOR COMMUNICATIVE COMPETENCE: SELLING IDEAS

We are speaking throughout about the need to develop communicative competence. A main way to do so is to think of the idea of selling ideas. There is nothing new in this idea: according to Pink (2012), to sell is human, and we all do it all the time. Whenever your child persuades you to go to see the latest blockbuster, or when your dog brings you its lead, you are being sold an idea. The question is, what persuades you to buy it? And, when it is your turn to sell someone an idea, such as when you write your report or dissertation in which you claim to have created your own theory of practice, how do you sell this idea to your reader?

The practice of selling is as old as the hills. There is also a substantial literature around it, including McDonnell and McNiff (2014), who outline how adopting an action research approach can help your professional selling practices. Here are some of the main principles of selling.

First, there is the process called AIDA. When selling something, you need to attract your prospective customer's *attention*, capture their *interest* and evoke their *desire* so that they will be prompted to take *action* (purchase your product). People use the same process when they want you to buy a car, go to a party or give them a degree. However, it is not the strategy itself so much as how you do it (the methodology) that makes the process work, and a core element is speaking directly to your purchaser (your reader, in your case). Here is what you do.

Practising AIDA in the production of a text

First, learn how to put AIDA into practice when you write, as follows:

Attention: attract your reader's attention

To attract your reader's attention you can:

Begin a story with a strong sentence

Some examples of stories that begin with a strong sentence are:

- From an essay:

> Here are two essays about what it means to be a foreigner. The first is set in Venice at the dawn of the sixteenth century, as the city became the seat of a global trading empire; many of the strangers necessary to run that empire

were unwanted in the city itself: Germans, Greeks, Turks, and Jews – Jews were the least wanted. What was it like to carve out a life in a hostile place? I asked myself this question when I first visited the Jewish ghetto of Venice in the 1960s.

(Sennett, 2011; academic book)

- From a dissertation:

This paper is an account of a self-study enquiry into my practice and a full expression of my living educational theory that has helped me gradually to develop into a better and more advanced individual. Throughout this research I have come to realize how important it is to hold values of social justice, honesty, respect, Ubuntu, love and empathy.

(Zola Malgas, 2009; dissertation)

Say something really interesting

Some examples of really interesting openings are:

- From a travel book:

For the past twenty years I have been writing with both hands. I thought: 'I'll write a few more pieces and then I'll work on my novel'.

(Paul Theroux, 1986)

- From a project report:

In the current climate of educational change in Ireland many guidance practitioners may be sceptical about participating in a process possibly perceived as having few benefits and requiring extra work in an environment where many feel demands exceed capacity to deliver. However, teaching and learning in Ireland is undergoing major reform. The paradigm of education is changing to an extent that will require teachers, and schools, to re-examine and re-imagine how and what they teach. Unless guidance counsellors adapt there may be little chance of preserving their roles and existence.

(Peter Hyde, 2013)

Interest: capture your reader's interest

How do you capture your reader's interest? You can do the following:

Pay attention to the underlying question, 'what's in it for me?'

When they pick up a text, any reader, including you, asks themselves questions such as these:

- Why should I spend time reading this?
- What are they trying to tell me?
- What right have they got to tell me anything?
- What are they trying to achieve?
- Why is it an issue?
- Why should I read this?

It is your job to engage with these questions. The first thing is to make the story sound interesting.

Make the story sound interesting

You can make a story sound interesting only if you are interested in it yourself. You can demonstrate your interest by writing in a lively, engaging manner, varying your language and adopting a reader-friendly tone. Compare the two extracts below:

- 'The research, undertaken from 2015 to 2016, showed that patients responded to personal interactions.'
- 'In my research, which lasted from 2015 to 2016, I wanted to find ways of engaging patients in their own well-being. I found that personal engagement led to interactions that patients found meaningful.'

Write in a reader-friendly style

Sometimes, students on academic courses feel that they have to write in 'Sunday-best' language, which is not the case. 'Use' is as good as, if not better than, 'utilise'. Aim to speak directly to your reader, with no fuss, aware that you are speaking with an educated reader who wants to know what you have done and how you have contributed to knowledge of the field. It is your responsibility to tell them, clearly and to the point.

Desire: evoke your reader's desire to know more

It is important to evoke your reader's desire to know more in order to keep their attention throughout and keep them on your side. You can do this using the following strategies.

Give them advance notices and summaries

You can keep your reader focused on your text by providing advance organisers at the beginning of a chapter or section. You can say, 'This section deals with the following points . . .', and list the points you will be writing about. This strategy also keeps you on track.

Give them signposts and clues and drop hints

Signposts keep your reader's attention. They usually take the form of headings and subheadings, written in different fonts and weights. They also take the form of link sentences and easy transitions, using words such as 'therefore' and 'it follows that . . .'. This is especially important when you are developing an argument.

Remember that you are writing an academic text, not a novel. In a novel, you hide the signposts and manipulate the text to provide information: 'She glanced at the clock' carries as much meaning as, 'She was nervous and wanted to get away from the meeting quickly'. You save the findings ('whodunnit') until the last page. In an academic text, you reveal all on the first page: you say what the work is about and set out the main findings. You write: 'In this paper I wish to explain how I have generated my personal theory of dentistry practice.' Follow the mantra, 'Tell your reader what you are going to say, say it, and then tell them what you have said.' Ignore the timeworn phrase, 'It speaks for itself'. It doesn't.

Summarise as you go

It can be useful to pause at points in your text, especially after a long stretch, and summarise what you have said. This gives you and your reader a short breathing space and also helps to consolidate previous material before you move on to the next point. Remember that it is your responsibility to walk with your reader through your text and not let them get lost.

Action: *prompting your reader to action*

How do you get your reader to want to read your text? Do the following:

- Write clearly and coherently and speak directly to your reader. Write in a plain, uncluttered way. Avoid using words such as 'highly' or 'extremely', unless you are using them to make a point. Avoid hyperbole, the kind of exaggeration that invites exclamation marks. Do not write 'It was fantastic!!'
- Be modest. Do not write, 'surely . . .' or 'obviously . . .', as if the point you are making is self-evident. Do not say, 'My report contains ideas that no one has ever thought of before'. Well, maybe so, but your reader will not warm to you.
- Avoid repetition. Check throughout your manuscript that you have not used the same piece of text twice. Keep a list of favourite references and check them off once you have used them.
- Use correct grammar and punctuation. This means proofreading your text many times before submitting it and checking that all your references are correct and intact.
- Make your manuscript look attractive. Break up the page with white space by using section headings, bullet points and other typographical

devices. Avoid presenting a page full of solid text – enough to put off even the most stalwart reader. Choose a font that looks lively and inviting but not flowery. Cut out all embroidery: your text has to stand on its own feet, without embellishment.

These and many other strategies will ensure that your reader will find reading your text an engaging experience and will inspire them to read it. However, you still need to do more, and this moves us into the methodology of selling.

Practising the methodology of the sale: the process of communication

Selling an idea involves the following:

Establish your own credibility

Aim to present yourself as someone who knows their stuff. This means knowing your subject matter as well as methodological matters. It means showing that you appreciate the need for clear communication through the way you speak and organise your text. Your reader wants to feel they are not wasting their time by reading a text that is unsure of its ground, so aim to project yourself as a confident, knowledgeable person who has researched the field and whose ideas are to be taken seriously. This means, however, that you need to spend time doing the necessary preparatory work. Readers quickly pick up a tone from a text and can tell whether or not the author is genuine.

Establishing your credibility also means speaking with your own voice. Although it can be helpful to learn from other writers (see Chapter 5), you should also develop your own style and form of speaking and have confidence in what you are saying. This takes time and practice, and links with issues of self-identity (as page 68). Have confidence that you are able to do research and articulate what you know, and also project a sense that you find your own ideas exciting and wish to share them with others to get their feedback.

Approach the writing as establishing a dialogue with your reader

Always keep your reader in mind and talk with them, as if they are there with you in the room (they will be when they read your work). Don't just go on about an idea without checking that your reader will understand it and be willing to engage with you. For example, if you use a specialised word such as 'ipsative', explain it to your reader. Also, if you write a complex sentence, add an accompanying sentence to explain what you mean. Better still, break the text up into smaller, easily digestible sentences so that your reader will be able to follow your arguments easily.

Anticipate your reader's needs

Always check whether you have explained the contexts you are writing about to your reader. Do not say, 'We were discussing ideas about organisational development. The visit to Scotland was especially interesting. But the organisational development issue took up all our discussion time.' Unless you have already told your reader about the visit to Scotland, they will be left wondering, 'Where did that come from? What is its relevance to the issue?' This is a common blip among new researchers – they assume that their reader knows what they are talking about, which is not necessarily the case. All your reader knows is what you tell them on the page.

Make sure you know your reader's context and background

Always write for a reader as if you know them. To a certain extent, this may be the case: you know your academic supervisor or your examiner, possibly not personally, but you do know what they will bring to the task of reading your text. Write for them from your understanding of their experience. This means being clear in advance how your work will be assessed and what their expectations are of you. It is largely a case of producing an authoritative text that is written for the professional and academic field you are working in, but it is also a case of appreciating that readers have specific expectations of your text and delivering what they are looking for.

Provide signposts, give clues and drop hints

As discussed earlier, signposts, clues and hints can help a reader to understand and interpret what you are saying without difficulty. However, providing them means stepping away from what you are saying (the content space) and thinking about how you are saying it (moving into the communications space), to check that you are writing for your reader and keeping them with you. You can do this by using a range of devices to let your reader see where they are in the text. Give them reminders about what your argument is by providing summaries. Give them advance notice of what is coming next. Your reader may not even notice that you are doing this, but the fact that you do it will make sure they have a good reading experience and they will warm to you. Ginger Rogers once said to Fred Astaire, 'Why do you practise so much?', to which he replied, 'To make it look easy'. This is what you should do: make it look easy, even though it may not be. But it is your work, so you should spend time and effort on it and be confident that it is the best you can do, not the second best.

Present your work in a way appropriate for your reader

It can help if you package your text in a way appropriate to your reader's context. If you are writing a dissertation, aim to set out your text as per institutional guidelines: so many words per page, specific dimensions of the text on the page, the text justified (the edges go down the page in a straight line, not ragged), word count on the first page, and so on. If you are sending work to colleagues or an academic supervisor, put your name on the file and date it (supervisors will be receiving texts from ten others labelled 'Module 3', so they need guidance in identifying which is which). Aim to present an error-free text, with a full and accurate list of references. Be aware always of the need to make the reading task easy for your reader. It may not get you extra marks, but it will definitely incline your reader to read your work today rather than tomorrow. Besides, it is a sign of your own professional standards.

Invite your reader to develop the conversation

You may not see the delivery of your text as the end of the relationship with your reader, and this is a powerful stance to take. If appropriate, invite your reader to continue the conversation, possibly as a developmental conversation through emails or a blog. In this way, you and your reader could continue to co-construct knowledge. This would be an exciting thing to do, but don't be disappointed if they do not take up the opportunity. Just be content that you have produced a high-quality text that you can be proud of and that will do justice to your research.

In conclusion, be confident that, by trying out the principles of AIDA, you stand a good chance of ensuring that your reader will read your text with great interest and enjoyment. Above all, approach the writing of your text with enjoyment: it will strike a chord in your reader that they will find most attractive and lead them to read your work with an open and attentive mind.

Summary

This chapter has considered some aspects of what is involved in communicating with others and how you can learn to do so: that is, how you can develop communicative competence. Core aspects involve distinguishing between writing for a reader and reading like a reader, which is when you read for information, and learning to read like a writer, which involves issues of thinking of yourself as a writer, understanding how you position your reader in relation to yourself, and developing the capacity to critique your own thinking. The chapter also offers advice on the idea of selling ideas and how to practise the invaluable technique of AIDA.

We now move to Part II and the idea of what is involved in learning to be a writer. This issue forms the content of Chapter 5, especially how engaging with the literatures may be understood as a key part of this.

Part II

Writing and producing a text

This part is about writing and producing a text. These are action phases in an overall action enquiry, where you aim to transform your earlier thinking and planning into the reality of a text.

Writing a text may be organised into different activities, and these are outlined in Chapters 5–7.

Chapter 5 is about learning to be a writer. It explains the importance of developing a writer's identity along with all your other identities and how you can achieve this. Part of the process is to read, so the chapter includes advice about engaging with the literatures. This takes on a double perspective: how you learn to write through reading like a reader (reading for information) and through reading like a writer (where you learn from studying how writers write).

Chapter 6 is about the writing process. This is explained as different phases (or practices) within the wider practice of producing a text. The phases are planning, composing, and editing and revising.

Chapter 7 is about writing a report or a dissertation. Different frameworks and structures are offered for how to write an action research text, from a fairly rigid form to a flexible narrative form.

Examples are taken throughout from the published work of action researchers in different contexts, to show how they have developed their own ideas and written in their own styles, while producing high-quality texts and achieving full recognition for their work.

Chapter 5

Learning to be a writer: engaging with the literatures

This chapter is about learning to be a writer. Writing is closely linked with reading, like two sides of the same coin. Further, learning to be a writer means being aware of the links between reading and writing, and the place that reading takes in your studies. In many ways, you learn to write through reading.

In academic terms, people tend to refer to reading as 'engaging with the literatures'. This engagement is compulsory for any higher education course that rightly requires participants to show that they have read widely and appropriately. Also, 'engaging' means critical engagement – that is, not just reading and producing summaries of what authors say, but also questioning, agreeing with or possibly disagreeing with what they say, as well as how they say it, and learning from the experience. This means that, when you engage critically with an author's work, you learn both from what they say and from what they do as they say it.

Developing this dual focus means appreciating that you can read for different purposes. You can learn from what authors say, in which case you read for information (you read like a reader), and you can also learn from what they do when they write, in which case you learn how to improve your writing practices (you read like a writer).

This chapter focuses on these two different, though connected, elements and is organised in the following sections:

- Reading for information: reading like a reader
- Reading to learn how to improve writing practices: reading like a writer

To see the difference between reading like a reader and reading like a writer, consider this passage from poet and critic Allen Tate:

> There are many ways to read, but generally speaking there are two ways. They correspond to the two ways in which we may be interested in a piece of architecture. If the building has Corinthian columns, we can trace the origin and

development of Corinthian columns; we are interested as historians. But if we are interested as architects, we may or may not know about the history of the Corinthian style; we must, however, know all about the construction of the building, down to the last nail or peg in the beams. We have got to know this if we are going to put up buildings ourselves.

(Tate, 1940: 506; cited in Bunn, 2011: 74)

It is the same when one is writing a text, including an academic text. You produce content, which includes the research story; this is the equivalent of ensuring that columns are Corinthian and not Ionic or Doric. You also construct a text, which involves understanding the different structures and frameworks that hold the text together and how one element links with another; this is the equivalent of ensuring that nails and pegs are in place. Both aspects are necessary for successful writing and both can be learned from a focused study of other people's and your own writing.

First, then, consider what is involved when you engage with the literatures from the perspective of reading for information, that is, reading like a reader.

READING FOR INFORMATION: READING LIKE A READER

When you read like a reader, you read the literatures for different kinds of information and insight. In an academic context, these aims include:

- to find out what other people have already said about your topic;
- to test your findings and ideas against those of key authors;
- to develop your own arguments and points of view.

Finding out what other people have already said about your topic

When you write your report or dissertation, you need to show that you understand both the topic itself and its contexts.

Showing that you understand the topic means reading widely about it. The topic (or substantive issue, or subject matter) could be the manufacture of cars, the construction of houses or a person-centred form of pedagogy. You would first need to engage with the professional literatures: these can be scholarly articles such as those you find in refereed journals, as well as books or trade magazines. You would read about, say, the manufacture of cars as well as the methodology of action research (see Example 16, on page 101).

You study the literatures to check what other people have already said about the topic you are writing about. This provides contextual information for your own treatment of the topic. You can, of course, cover the same ground as other people, or you may adopt a different stance to what is usually said in the literatures. In this case, you would need to show, by comparison with other texts, how your ideas might be shown as different and (you hope) more appropriate for the field (see Example 17, on page 101).

Example 16

In her study of organisational culture, Miriam Judge (2000: 205) said that:

> Of all the literature surveyed, Schein's (1992) *Organizational Culture and Leadership* provided the most simulating and thought provoking analysis of the subject. By challenging my own narrow interpretation of organisational culture as a 'structural construct', Schein greatly influenced my research approach, inquiry method and subsequent analysis of findings.

Example 17

Julie Pearson (2015) gives a detailed account of the physical education literatures to contextualise her study of her practice as a PE lecturer in Initial Teacher Education and also to make her own position about PE clear. She writes:

> The inclusion of Physical Education (PE) as a compulsory subject within the primary and secondary curriculum highlights the value of learning within the subject area, as PE remains the only subject that focuses on the body, physical development and learning in, through and about the physical (DES, 1991). Alongside physical competencies, PE is a context for and means of learning a wide range of valuable skills such as cognitive and critical skills, aesthetic judgement, decision making and social skills (Bell and Penney, 2004). These attributes emphasise freedom of thinking, which is removed from the obvious physical learning within PE, offering a pragmatic, emancipatory view of education. Talbot (2001) claims that as an academic subject, PE helps children to respect their bodies, contributes towards the integrated development of the mind and the body and positively enhances self-confidence and self-esteem. As a successful sports person and PE teacher, I have experienced the positive learning experiences Talbot (2001) suggests, but a high proportion of those I teach do not possess such a view of PE. A lack of confidence in their own practical ability, their negative feeling towards PE and low self-esteem within a mainly practical subject is at the heart of this thesis. The understanding I have gained from doing the research suggests ways to improve the learning experiences for trainee teachers and to offer a different view of learning within PE to combat a behaviourist, outcomes-oriented view of PE. The literature review provides a building base for my research to critique in order to understand the subject as a whole and the 'hidden connections' (Capra, 2002) it offers.

Engaging with the literatures like this enables Julie to demonstrate what she has learned from other authors and also to test her ideas against those of key authors. This is an important idea, as follows.

Testing your ideas against those of key authors

Testing your ideas against the ideas of others is essential. It is no good saying that you have come up with innovative ideas unless you can show in what way they are innovative, or different from what other people already say. You need to have read around your chosen area to be able to say these things. Your area can be substantive (topic or subject) issues (PE in Julie's example above) or process issues, such as developing new ways of doing things.

It is also important, as noted in Chapter 4, to establish your credibility when presenting your text. You need to reassure your reader that your knowledge is up to date and factually correct, as well as appropriate for the field.

Example 18

Jonathan Vincent (2015: 1) describes how he created 'a participatory workshop' where, he says, 'a dialogic space was established such that the voices of students with Asperger's Syndrome could be "heard" by using critical autobiographical extracts about teaching and learning at university'.

He explains how his research is innovative by referring to what he calls 'the "disability" literatures':

> Over the last two decades higher education institutions have made significant steps towards becoming more inclusive learning environments for all students and in particular for disabled students. Significant milestones were the introduction of the Disability Discrimination Act (1995), the Special Educational Needs and Disability Act (2001) and later the Equality Act (2010), which were implemented to end the discrimination that disabled students faced by securing funding and the right to provision of reasonable and anticipatory adjustments. However, disabled students still largely remain marginalised within this discourse and their voices unheard; thus 'good practice' is often imposed *on them* rather than informed *by them*.

By producing a text like this, Jonathan shows that he speaks with the authority of empirical knowledge of the field, so his words are to be taken seriously, even though a reader may disagree with the stance he takes.

Developing your own arguments and points of view

As noted throughout, when you write your report or dissertation, you say what you have learned through doing your research: this means that you make a claim to knowledge. You can say that you have discovered knowledge (something that other people already knew) or that you have created knowledge (something that no one else knew, so that your claim to knowledge is original). At doctoral level, any knowledge claim must be original, but, for undergraduate- or master's-level studies, the claim need not be original. Whatever the case may be, the ideas you write about are your own ideas, and you decide the stance you adopt. This means that you need to stand by your own opinions and views and justify them. Unless you can justify why you have come to certain conclusions, you cannot expect other people to take your opinion seriously, let alone agree with you. Again, this means showing how your ideas are the same as or different from the ideas already available in the literatures.

Example 19

It can be really interesting to follow debates in the literatures themselves, where one author takes issue with another or with a commonly held view; for example, Christopher Branson *et al.* (in preparation) write about the need for what they call 'transrelational leadership', which is different from conventional forms of leadership.

> Our starting point for re-inventing a theory of leadership so that the nature and practice of middle leadership could be conceived as a singularly coherent phenomenon was a critique of how it has been traditionally defined. Although there is no universally accepted definition of leadership, Yukl's (2006) view is commonly applied and states that leadership is 'the process of influencing others to understand and agree about what needs to be done and how to do it, and the process of facilitating individual and collective efforts to accomplish shared objectives' (p. 8). We contend that such a definition of leadership directs us towards the product of leadership rather than its enactment. This suggests that leadership theory has concentrated too much on the behavioural characteristics of leadership and has overlooked the more fundamental relational requirements.

Now, let's move from considering the importance of engaging with the literatures and consider what you do when you read like a reader.

What do you do when you read like a reader?

When you read like a reader, you read a text closely in order to work out what the author is meaning. According to Peha (n.d.), you do the following:

- *Ask questions*. You ask questions about what you read: why things are happening like this, what characters are doing, what words and sentences actually mean – anything that you are not sure of.
- *Predict*. Readers make guesses about what is about to happen next. They guess what the next word or idea will be. 'Predicting', says Peha, 'helps readers sort out important information from unimportant information. It helps them organize their thinking as they encounter new material.'
- *Infer*. We all tend to come to conclusions about things, without having to be told, and we like to work things out for ourselves. Perhaps this is the fascination of doing crossword puzzles. Good writers, says Peha, leave clues for readers to discover important information. Writers of detective novels leave hints and clues along the storyline to help you work out whodunit. Agatha Christie always deliberately misled her readers, though: she laid a trail of clues but then sprang a surprise at the end by showing the clues to be red herrings.
- *Connect*. When we read a text, we are reminded of our own lives. We connect similar personal episodes with what we read, and look for patterns and relationships in the events being told.
- *Feel*. Reading a text can evoke specific feelings in a reader. We feel sad at sad intervals in the text, and happy when things go right for the actors. When you write, be aware that you also can evoke these feelings in your reader. This means that you need to find ways of evoking the right kinds of feeling that will encourage your reader/examiner to award you a pass.
- *Evaluate*. When you read, you make judgements about what you are reading. You decide whether it is good or not and whether you should continue reading or how seriously you should take the text (adapted from Peha, n.d.).

You also think about what effect the text is having on you. Does reading the text give you a feeling of excitement? Do you pick up the text because you can't wait to turn the next page? Or not? All these ideas about what readers do when they read are important for you. You are writing a text to be read by a reader who is a real-life person. Like you, they experience demands on their time, have a limited concentration span and get frustrated when they read typographical errors. As a writer, it is in your interests always to consider what it means to be a reader and to read like a reader. You also need to think about what may be going through your reader's mind when they read your text.

Now consider what is involved in doing a literature review, which is an aspect of the practice of reading like a reader.

Doing a literature review

Most research-method textbooks advise you to do a literature review. However:

> Although opinions differ about the extent of literature review needed before a study begins, qualitative texts (e.g., Creswell, 2003; Marshall & Rossman, 2006) refer to the need to review the literature so that one can provide the rationale for the problem and position one's study within the ongoing literature about the topic.
>
> (Creswell, 2007: 102)

This would definitely be an expectation in a social sciences report, but it can vary in an action research report. Personally, I think it is essential to do a literature review of some kind, for the reasons stated above, and also because it provides a context for your research. You are able to spell out the social, cultural and historical contexts and especially the policy contexts for your area through referring to policy documents (as Jonathan Vincent does above). You may, however, choose to do several smaller reviews throughout your report, depending on how long it is. For a 40,000-word dissertation, it would be reasonable to spend about 3,000–4,000 words on a literature review, whereas, in a report of about 10,000 words you would produce a much shorter one. Another acceptable, and expected, strategy would be to engage throughout with key issues and debates, almost like mini-reviews, and to reference authors at all points of the text (which is what has been done in this book too). This means that you show engagement with the literatures throughout your text. For example, Chris Glavey (2008) chose to do a review of the leadership literatures as a dedicated chapter of his thesis to situate his study of his own leadership (see www.jeanmcniff.com/items.asp?id=44). More often, however, instead of a single big review, you may spread your literature review across your text, possibly as small reviews. Or you may choose to develop a specific argument at a particular point in your text, supported by relevant literatures (see Examples 20 and 21, on page 106).

There are no hard and fast rules about this, but you do need to show critical engagement and give good contextualised reasons for why you have chosen to address your preferred topic.

Organising your literature review

Aim to organise your literature review to address some key questions, including the following:

- What is the current state of knowledge and who are the key writers, researchers and experts in this field?
- What different definitions, concepts and issues are relevant to this topic?
- How has thinking/knowledge about this topic changed over the years?

Example 20

Josephine Bleach (2013: 17) develops a specific argument as she shows the importance of her work in developing community action research. She writes:

> Community action research, with its emphasis on building cross-organisational learning communities to undertake action research projects (Senge and Scharmer, 2001), was chosen as our research methodology as it encouraged bottom–up, flexible, continuous and cooperative change. As we believe that successful implementation depends on changing behavior (Medical Research Council [MRC] 2008), we hope to improve our educational practices collectively, by thinking differently, acting differently and relating to one another differently (Kemmis, 2009). A cumulative approach to knowledge generation (Blamey and Mackenzie, 2007) is taken, where learning accumulates slowly within and across evaluation rather than delivering 'big bang' answers to questions of programme effectiveness.

Example 21

Colin O'Connor (2015) also develops a specific argument as he writes about his work of encouraging former offenders to gain meaningful work or additional qualifications, as follows:

> Statistical information provides us with evidence of the high levels of disadvantage experienced by former offenders in the labour market. Research evidence suggests that isolation from employment and educational pathways significantly increases the likelihood of initial offending (Nally, Lockwood, Ho and Knutson, 2014). Without gaining employment, it is estimated that around 50% of ex-offenders will return to prison within three years of being released (Gonzalez, 2012). Yet the government green paper 'Reducing Re-offending through Skills and Employment' (2005) claims that the employment prospects of ex-offenders are well below those of the community in general.

- What are the different (and sometimes conflicting) theories associated with this topic?
- What are the key points of disagreement in the existing literature?
- What are the unanswered questions/problems associated with the topic and what does the literature say about any attempts to tackle them?

- What are the main directions for future research/knowledge development in this area?
- How will any of the research that you might attempt yourself position itself within the existing literature?

(Moore and Murphy, 2005: 120–1)

Similarly, Walliman and Buckler (2008: 212) recommend doing a literature review for the following reasons:

- It ensures that you have properly briefed yourself beforehand, and that you are fully aware of what other research exists in your chosen field. In the context of some courses, you will be expected to outline the theoretical issues that link up with your chosen topic.
- It enables you to discuss the strengths and weaknesses of what other people have done and reflect on the relevant field of knowledge.
- It provides an established framework to which you can refer in order to indicate the extent to which you have drawn on previously published work for the design of your own project.
- It allows you to comment on aspects of your own methodology (in comparison with what others have done) or set your eventual findings alongside those already reported in the literature.

Murray (2002: 103) also says that a review should serve the following purposes:

- to give an overview of the 'big issues';
- to select some of these for your studies;
- to summarise other people's work;
- to evaluate other people's work;
- to provide a context for your own work;
- to identify gaps;
- to develop an understanding of theory and method.

Here are some important points to bear in mind when doing a literature review for any kind of research text, including an action research text.

A literature review is not simply a list of texts with descriptions of contents. This kind of writing is more like a catalogue that you search to find what you are looking for. A reader of this kind of review could just as easily read an annotated list of references at the back of a report. A literature review is a more in-depth engagement with key texts that have informed your thinking and writing.

Remember that certain golden rules about the literatures are non-negotiable. These are:

- Always reference ideas you get from other people and give your sources of quotations (Julian Stern, of York St John University, says that

from a builder you get a quote: from the literature you get a quotation).
If you take people's ideas and pass them off as your own, or lift words
directly out of texts without acknowledging your source, you are
committing plagiarism. Plagiarism is a serious offence. If you are caught
out, it could mean that your work will not be accepted and, in more
serious cases, that you will no longer be accepted on your programme.

- Do not name drop. Do not use Foucault's name unless you have read
  the primary sources (that is, texts written by Foucault, not texts about
  Foucault and his works, which are called secondary sources). You may
  find that your reviewer is a Foucault expert and would like to talk
  with you further about what you quote from Foucault, which may be
  bad news for you. So, avoid what Bassey (1999) calls 'king-making',
  which is to drop names, or 'sand-bagging', which is to pad out a text
  with extra words that don't actually contribute to the meaning of
  the text.

Finally, look on your engagement with the literatures as having a
conversation with authors, living and dead. Here is a lovely passage that
communicates this idea, from Nahil al-Tikriti, who tells a story while
'roam[ing] the stacks of one of the world's truly great libraries':

> Instead of seeing the usual information-packed inanimate objects lying on shelves,
> I suddenly envisaged a cacophony of passionate debates, insults, romances,
> genocide defenses, patriarchy justifications, and all the other phenomena one
> might find in such a vessel filled with millions of texts in hundreds of languages.
> As they were organized both topically and regionally, that night the books on
> my floor of specialization harangued me in shelving blocs – fiery Albanian
> nationalists here, pious Hanafi jurisprudents two rows across, followed by stern
> Ottoman apologists and whispering Sufi sensualists. I pondered what the
> complete absence of such books would mean. At least the cacophony would end
> – but what then?
>
> (2010: 93)

Although your aim is probably not to join the ranks of writers like these,
your aim is definitely to get your award, so here is some practical advice
about strategies for doing a literature review.

How to do a literature review

Approach doing your literature review in a systematic way. Finding sources
is called 'a literature search', and there are simple strategies for doing this,
including the following:

Start, as noted, by finding out what has been said on your topic. You
can do this by jotting down your own ideas and beginning to focus on
specific areas that are relevant to your topic. For example, within the field

of management studies, you may wish to focus on a specific area, such as conducting staff meetings or negotiating with employees.

You can search for sources in a range of ways, including the following:

- *Use the Internet.* Many online resources are available, such as Google Scholar. Do be careful though: you will find a lot of information, some of it useful, some useless and some faulty, if not downright incorrect, so use these sources with discretion. Also, be careful of Wikipedia. Although it is a wonderfully informative resource most of the time, it can contain misleading information, given that it is an open resource, which means that anyone (informed or not) can contribute. More useful perhaps are the following:
- *Search your library's databases.* Ask the staff for help in finding key texts. They will also be able to help you refine your search and zoom in on exactly what you are looking for.
- *Read journals.* These tend to contain articles that provide the most up-to-date information on a topic. Look carefully at the arguments they make and also look at the references lists. These will lead you on to other related issues.
- *Be clear about what area you wish to focus on in your study.* You could ask yourself: 'What specific area of management am I interested in? Am I looking for ideas about practical management styles or more abstract management theories? What is the context – industry or education?' Focusing like this can save you a lot of time and effort and keep you on track.
- *As well as referencing contemporary literatures, remember traditional foundation texts in the field.* To understand the entire field of action research you would definitely need to go back to Dewey and Freire, and probably also back to the Greeks, but be sensible and adjust your search according to the size of the task in hand.
- *Read your institution's online advice.* Most higher education institutions provide online support – see, for example, the University of Leicester's advice page at www2.le.ac.uk/offices/ld/resources/writing/writing-resources/literature-review. Do a comparison of the advice offered there and find what suits you.
- *Talk with colleagues about your work and ask them for advice.* You can do this by arranging an informal reading group or joining the group your supervisor perhaps organises. Arrange to meet with other course members in a reading group one lunchtime a week. Face-to-face discussion of ideas can provide a lot of information, as well as invaluable support.
- *Use social networking for the same purposes.* You can tweet core texts or useful quotations to valued friends and colleagues and build up a database of resources.

Keeping a reading journal

As well as keeping a learning journal, aim to keep a reading journal. Keep a list of any text you read and note the date when you read it. Write down a summary of what the text says and write out key points that you will use as quotations in your report. Always, always note the page number. When quoting from the literatures in your own text, you must give a page reference. You will lose marks if you do not. Do not ignore this advice!

Also aim to respond critically to what you read: that is, don't take what you read for granted, but develop an argument with yourself or an author about it. You can use your notes as data in your report or dissertation, to show how your ideas have developed and how you have engaged critically with the text and with your own thinking.

We now turn to working with the literatures and consider what it means to read like a writer.

READING TO LEARN HOW TO IMPROVE WRITING PRACTICES: READING LIKE A WRITER

We said above that you read like a reader mainly to get information about a text. As you read, you focus on what the writer is saying. However, when you read like a writer, you focus on how the writer writes, the different techniques they use, and how they communicate to you what they want you to hear.

Here is a story by Katie Ray Wood, similar to the one above by Allan Tate, about what it means to read like a writer.

> To illustrate this point I often tell students about my friend who is a very accomplished seamstress. I explain learning a craft from a craftsperson this way:
> Because my friend is a seamstress, she goes to the mall or to the dress shops differently than the rest of us who aren't seamstresses. First, it takes her a lot longer than a normal person to make her way through the store. She turns the dresses and jumpers and shirts inside out, sometimes sitting right down on the floor to study how something is made. While the rest of us mere shoppers are looking only at sizes and prices, my friend is looking closely at inseams and stitching and 'cuts on the bias.' She wants to know how what she sees was made, how it was put together. And the frustrating thing for anyone shopping with her is that as long as it takes her, she hardly ever buys anything! You see, my friend's not shopping for clothes, she's shopping for *ideas for* clothes. After a day at the mall she goes home with a head full of new ideas for what she might make next on her trusty sewing machine.
>
> (1999: 13; emphasis in original)

You should do the same when you read. Critical engagement in this case means looking at the language that authors use, looking at their use of words and thinking about how you can do the same.

Often, the idea of reading like a writer is new for many of us, and it can be difficult to see what it involves. The basic message, says Bunn (2011), is to appreciate that writers make choices when they write; they decide to use one word rather than another and weigh up the benefits of writing a sentence in a particular way. Reading their work and making yourself aware of the choices they make can help you also to make important decisions about how you write. From studying the writing of an author, you can learn which techniques best suit a text at a particular moment, or why one word is better than another. Reading then becomes a wonderful strategy for learning how to write.

Try this out with some of the extracts in this chapter so far. First, ask yourself these questions (go back to Chapter 2 and look at them there):

- What does the author wish to say?
- Who do they wish to say it to?
- How do they say it?
- Why do they say it that way?

Compare, for example, the texts by Christopher Branson *et al.* and the one by Josephine Bleach in this chapter, or look at any other case study material in the book. Is it clear what they wish to say from those extracts? Can you identify their audience? Look at how they say it: look at the choice of words and sentence structure, and how the sentences are put together. Why do you think they say it that way?

Now, look at how I have written this book. Think about the choices I have made in doing so. Why did I choose particular extracts from people's writing? Was it because the subject matter fitted the contexts? Or because they are written in different styles? Or because they all use language skilfully and economically to communicate complex messages? Or for other reasons?

Now, look at some writing you have done recently and ask yourself: 'How long did it take me to decide to use that particular word? What choices did I make in choosing that piece of text for my introduction? How many times did I revise the text to get the melody just right? How many times did I polish it?' (Richard Rorty is a great polisher. He says (2003: 179), 'I'm conscious of striving after turns of phrase and that kind of thing. I spend a lot of time polishing things up.') Also, remember that you are writing an academic text that aims to model the kinds of professionalism required in the field. Does your text work? Is it readable, while also establishing a firm academic base? [A moment's reflection: why have I just used the word 'firm'? I could also have used 'solid' or 'concrete' or 'hard'. What is special about the word 'firm'? Would any of the other words have worked? If so, why? If not, why not? How long did it take me to decide to use this word and not another one?]

It is by thinking through texts like this that you develop a sense of the sound of a sentence, the feel of a word. Writing is full of choices. Further, really fluent writing looks easy. Why did Fred Astaire practise so much? To make it look easy.

How to read like a writer

Here are some ideas about how you can learn to read like a writer. It may at first seem strange, but after a while you actually start noticing the construction of a text, and then you start doing it automatically.

You can learn from your reading by noticing and copying. By 'copying', I am not referring to plagiarism in any shape nor form, but I am recommending that you study good writing and notice how authors integrate advice such as that given in this book into their writing. Look at the extracts in this chapter, for example, and write a piece from your own work and experience that adopts the same structure. Look at how the authors shape their sentences and how they ensure that the rhythm and cadence of the words is right for the context, and then try to do the same with your own writing. In the book *Steal Like an Artist*, Kleon (2012) says that all art is a form of plagiarism. In *The Craftsman*, Sennett (2009) tells how apprentices would spend years studying from their masters before they were allowed to set out on their own. All teaching, in a way, is to encourage students to study the craft of their topic, to learn to think in a particular way and to produce work that bears their original stamp.

This is what it means to engage critically with a text. It is engaging critically with both what the author is saying and also how they are saying it and what you can learn from them. The work you produce is not simply copied from the work of an expert: it is modelled on the work. Go around an art gallery and you will see artists painting the picture they are observing. They are not copying the picture so much as studying the technique, learning from it through trying to do it and adapting it to their own experiences. Look at how Gaugin uses colour to achieve a certain effect or how Elvis uses his voice and volume to communicate a specific emotion. Observe and learn, and then try it yourself. You will never become another Gaugin or Elvis (they were unique, as we all are), but you can adapt and develop a technique they have used in your own work. This is also what happens in action research. You and colleagues study what you are doing individually and then share your knowledge. Through the sharing, you come to co-construct knowledge and learn anew from others' experience.

Here are some strategies for learning to read like a writer.

- Always read with a notebook (paper or electronic) to hand. Keep a note of what you are reading and the reference. Write out key sentences or sections from which you may quote in your own text. Always identify the page reference.
- Stop every so often and summarise what you have read in your own words. This can help you focus on key meanings and also help your interpretation of the author's ideas.

- Keep a record of your responses to the text. You could divide a page of your notebook in two and write on one side, 'What I have read' and on the other, 'Reflections on what I have read'. This provides a historical record of your reading that you can perhaps include in your writing to show the development of your thinking.
- Write a summary of each chapter. You could produce a PowerPoint presentation of the book for yourself, noting key themes on different slides. You can send these kinds of homemade resources to friends and colleagues, which is an excellent way of sharing information.
- Write on the text itself. My preferred way is to underline a passage in pencil (I would not deface a book permanently with a highlighter pen, though some people do). Respect your books and papers: they are good allies who want to support you in your reading and understanding.

Also, read widely and eclectically. It does not matter what you read, as long as you find it engaging and fulfilling, though there is also a requirement to read prescribed and recommended texts. Use novels and magazines as literature sources, as well as more conventional sources such as textbooks. Draw links and associations between what you are reading and your own work: this can enrich your text and lend additional depth to arguments. Above all, enjoy what you do and let the enjoyment speak for itself. Readers can learn and improve their work from studying your writing, too. You will never know the influence you might have on other people's thinking and work, but you may like to think that you have contributed somewhere along the line. Nice idea.

Summary

This chapter has considered some of what is involved in learning to be a writer. Two main aspects are considered: what it means to read like a reader, which is about reading for information; and what it means to read like a writer, which is about learning techniques and skills from studying how writers write. A core aspect of this is learning to engage with the literatures, both for what they say about your area and also for what you can learn from other writers.

We now turn to Chapter 6, which is about learning to produce a text and the different aspects involved in the overall writing process.

Chapter 6

Learning to produce a text: the writing process

You are now at the point of thinking about writing and producing a text to be submitted for approval by readers and examiners. This is not a difficult task, provided you approach it in a systematic way. This chapter provides ideas about how you can do this. It is arranged to talk about the different phases involved in the production of the text and is organised in two sections:

- Getting ready to write;
- Producing your text.

As noted throughout, the process of producing a text may be seen as an action enquiry. It follows the same principles of: identify an issue, think about how to engage with the issue, take action, watch what happens, evaluate its effectiveness and decide on a new action in light of the evaluation, which leads you to identify a new issue, and so on. Those visual diagrams on the Internet that represent the action enquiry process as a closed circle are highly misleading: doing action research is about moving into new forms strengthened by learning generated through engaging with earlier forms. It takes a spiral rather than circular form (as shown in Figure 1.2 on page 27).

The first step in your enquiry about how to produce a text, therefore, involves taking stock of what you are already doing and planning for new action.

GETTING READY TO WRITE

At this point in your enquiry, you are planning to write. Note that there are different kinds of planning. In Chapter 2, we considered the overall planning of your text, where you asked these kinds of question, along with lots of other ones:

- Will you have time to do the writing? When will you do it?
- Will you have space to do the writing? Where will you do it?

- What aspects might you need help with? Who can you ask?
- Will you have the resources to produce your text? Have you the right equipment? Paper and ink cartridges are costly. How will you budget for them?

Now, however, you are planning to produce a text and getting ready to write in a more focused way.

Planning is essential for good-quality writing. Aim to divide your time between: (1) thinking, researching the field, gathering material and ideas and organising your material and ideas; and (2) writing words on a page and reviewing and revising what you have written. You can waste a lot of time by leaping into the writing without thinking through beforehand what you are going to say. The more time you spend on planning and organising, the greater the chances of a good-quality first draft. Here are some ideas about what is involved in getting ready to write.

Getting ready to write

Getting ready to write involves the following:

Gather ideas and marshal your thinking about the topic

Check whether you already have enough ideas about your topic or if you need to gather more. If you do, find the necessary information through consulting books, searching the Internet and talking with colleagues. Access as many sources as possible within the time and energy available.

Always carry a notebook. Jot down ideas as they come to you. Do not leave this until later, because you will probably forget what they were. Take photos and use them for inspiration. Use social networking to get ideas and share them with friends. Whatever information or ideas you gather, file them and keep them for later. It is better at the planning phase to have too much material than too little, and you can always discard it later if it is not needed, or use it for another piece of writing.

Read: engage with the literatures

Read as much as you can about your topic. You can access a lot of useful secondary sources from the Internet or reviews, but, if you are serious about your studies, you will also read the primary sources. This can be time-consuming, so factor in reading time when you decide to register for your study programme. If you are not prepared to do the reading, don't register in the first place.

Spend time reading while you are getting ready to write. Do this for several reasons: it gets you into the right frame of mind, you are immersed in the language of your topic and you glean ideas from others who have written about the topic. Read at all stages of the writing process – when preparing to write; during the writing, when you need to refresh ideas; and after the event, when you check what you have written against what others in the literatures say. Also, read at any time and wherever convenient: on the bus or train, standing in a queue, waiting for the dinner to cook. You can pack a lot of reading into the odd 5 minutes.

Example 22

Anne-Lise Thoresen emphasises the need for reading throughout her research as a university-based professional educator in Norway, working with midwives in a practice setting who are seeking to improve their capacity for mentoring midwives. She writes:

> The aims of the research were to help midwives develop pedagogical practices in relation to midwifery students; and to promote greater cooperation between university-based lecturers, practice-based midwives, and midwifery students. To achieve the aims we developed a project structured as a series of university-based meetings for midwives followed by their meeting with mentoring midwifery students in a clinical practice setting – to date this has been going on for five months. During the university-based meetings we put in place a range of strategies, including reflective teams, lectures and seminars, reading groups, and logs as a form of reflective writing. The analysis of the logs became a key aspect of the research, because from the transcripts it was possible to identify four levels of analysis:
>
> 1   Writing up as a record of activities at the end of the day (reflections on learning achieved during the activities above).
> 2   Part of my work as lead co-researcher was to transcribe the learning logs to form one common narrative, which I then emailed to all participants before the next university-based meeting. This meeting then began with a discussion about the narrative and the new knowledge that midwives had generated from their interim experience of mentoring the student midwives in the clinical setting.
> 3   (Current work) My identification and extraction of common themes emerging from the analysis of the common narrative which I will then discuss and negotiate with a group of critical friends.
> 4   Writing up a research report and sharing significant ideas.
>
> This research is potentially significant in that it contributes to new practices about learning logs as a means of professional education for midwives, and also to new thinking about the role of midwives as mentors in clinical practice settings.
>
> (Thoresen, 2011)

Organise yourself

Organise yourself and your resources and get ready for the job ahead. Things you need to think about include the following:

What are you good at, and where do you need help?

Do an analysis of what you are good at and where you may need further help. Most institutions offer workshops dealing with specific topics, so attend as many of these as possible. Find out if any writing retreats are available and sign up for them. Check out if an identified member of staff offers individual support and contact them. Ask the help desk in your resources centre about this kind of information or anything else they provide. Many resource centres organise 'Using the library' or 'Accessing information' sessions. Find out what support there is (this is part of your research) and then avail yourself of it.

What is your preferred mode of writing?

Some people like writing longhand, and some prefer writing directly on a computer. Many people mix and match. You may find that you prefer writing longhand when working out ideas and then move to a computer when writing them down. Be critical when writing first ideas immediately on a computer: when something appears in print, it can look good and have an air of authority, and you may be misled into thinking that you have achieved a great first draft when in fact you haven't (yet).

Gathering the tools of your trade

Make sure you have everything you need for your writing task. This includes:

- pens and pencils;
- notebooks;
- a computer: most institutions expect your work to be typed on a computer (also, if possible, learn how to type using all your fingers and practise typing to get confidence);
- a printer and copy paper (don't forget spare ink cartridges): although some institutions are moving towards web-based material for assignments and dissertations, it remains the case that most still want work presented as typescripts;
- a dictionary for checking spellings and meanings: use a dictionary as well as a spellchecker, which you cannot always trust, especially because most spellcheckers default to American spelling rather than UK;
- a thesaurus for finding synonyms and checking correct meanings;
- a desk or table to write on: use the writing spaces supplied by your institution as and when necessary;

- a personal library of core texts: you should buy these and not rely on library loans; remember that you can get second-hand books from web-based stores at a fraction of their original cost.

Understand your own habits and routines

Aim to build up and understand your own habits and routines and be confident about these. What works for others may not work for you, so be clear about what works for you and stick with it. Here are some of the most important habits and routines to cultivate.

Best time of day for working

Decide what the best time of day is for you to work. Morning or evening? Any time? Also, decide how long you can concentrate for and organise your time accordingly. Some people work in sporadic bursts; others in long periods of concentration. You may find that you work in short bursts when you are getting into the routine of writing but, when the ideas begin to flow, you can spend much longer at it.

Know when you need a break

Take breaks as and when you need. You will find that a short break refreshes you, even though you may feel you don't need one. During your break, do something completely different from your study, such as washing up or phoning a friend. Some people find it is better to take many short breaks than one long one during a study session, because it helps them stay on their toes for a longer period of time overall.

Don't neglect other work

It is important to keep up with other work, so divide your day into slots that you allocate to different tasks. Try to respond to emails regularly; if you leave them, they will simply mount up. Consult your tutor or the Internet for ideas on how to handle emails and use applications to help you organise them on your computer.

Stay healthy

It is important to take care of your health when studying and writing. Useful advice is as follows:

Sit properly at your desk

It is a common complaint that people's legs and shoulders often cramp and stiffen if they sit for too long in the same position. Check your own sitting position to see if your entire body is comfortable. If you work from home a lot, invest in a good chair that will give you proper support. Aim to change position regularly, perhaps every 20 minutes or so. Stand frequently. Ideally, get a sit–stand desk, but, if this is unrealistic, put your computer on an upside-down crate or on a pile of books, so that you can alternate standing and sitting as you type.

Get up and move around

Bend and stretch to keep muscles moving and to get oxygen to your entire body. This will feed back into your brain and keep you alert for longer. Go out into the garden and get some air.

Drink plenty of water

For hydration and keep a small bowl of water on your desk (but not near your computer or keyboard).

Take regular exercise

Go for walks and play tennis, or whatever game you play. Go and watch a football match. Staying active will keep you healthy and your mood high. There is no substitute for exercise, whether you spend frequent or long periods of time on it.

Reward yourself

When you think you have done a good job (but not otherwise), give yourself a chocolate or watch a TV programme. Using gentle strategies like this helps and sustains you through a task that at times can get tedious, even for the most experienced and dedicated of writers. Find out what works best for you, and do it.

Organise your time

Decide on the overall time available for writing up your project. Many small-scale research projects are estimated to be 100-hour projects. This means you

Table 6.1 Timeline for completing text in 3 months

Month	Task
January	Draw up action plan for study and writing; organise tools; consult core texts; meet with supervisor; meet with critical friends
	Check whether sufficient ideas; organise writing tools; begin gathering data and organising data base
	Start writing: aim to complete Introduction in draft
February	Write Part I of assignment in draft; consult with supervisor and solicit their feedback
	Produce Part II in draft; send out to critical friends
	Read as and when necessary
March	Fill in as per your own schedule.

have to arrange those hours into different jobs, including research time, reading time, reflecting time and writing time. To help you do this, work out a timeline, as in Table 6.1. The plan is for a notional 100-hour module, lasting 3 months, with a written assignment. You would adjust your timeline and tasks according to the writing assignment in hand.

When you have drawn up your timeline, then draw up an action plan, as in Table 6.2.

As well as drawing up plans like these, set yourself targets, including so many words per day and so many chapters per month. The most effective way of producing an extended text is to write a piece per day. Aim for a realistic output. Know what you can easily achieve and then try to write another 100 words.

You can also set study goals and writing goals. Murray (2002) recommends setting yourself targets of the form, 'By this time tomorrow I will have completed the Introduction to Chapter 2'. Aim to work in a steady, systematic way. Avoid bursts of writing with long gaps between. Try to stay in touch with your text: if you leave it even for a day, you will forget what you were saying and will have a hard time reconnecting.

As well as drawing up action plans, keep a calendar and appointments diary. Make sure you stay up to date with other events and don't let the writing take over your life.

Stay on top of the work

Aim to stay on top of the work. It can be difficult to catch up once you lose touch and momentum. Here are some strategies for doing so:

- Aim to meet all deadlines. If the idea of deadlines puts you off, think instead of start dates. If you haven't already done something, negotiate with yourself or your supervisor when you will start.
- Start before you are ready. If you wait until you are ready, you will never start. Just start. Also, don't worry about starting at the beginning. Start in the middle: in life, we are always in the middle of something and end up in the middle of something else. We never get to a starting point or

Table 6.2 Notional action plan for completing a text in 3 weeks

Week	Action	Done?	If not, when?
1	Preparation: revisit core texts; consult notes; consult tutor; read criteria for assignment; organise writing tools; cancel party on Monday	Yes	
2	Write for 2 hours each day; supplement with additional reading; check access to online library resources	Not yet.	Beginning April
3	Fill in as per your own schedule.		

an end point. Just start and let the writing take care of itself, as it will. The logic of the writing will make itself clear to you as you write.

- If you feel it would help, go on a writing retreat (though these do not suit everyone). If you do, be prepared to be told when to write and when to stop. The support of other people who are doing the same thing can help.
- If you run out of time, and all else fails, ask for a suspension of studies or an extension. Your institution has the facility for these, but keep them for real emergencies.

Producing and storing your work

Aim to keep your work organised as you do it. Draw up a physical or electronic project file. Keep files on your computer organised, name them clearly and put them into appropriate folders. Colour-coding your files can be useful – blue for first draft, mauve for second, red for final draft, or whatever suits your sense of colour. Always date your file and give it a name. It can be difficult to remember on which date a file was created, especially when you have twenty on your desktop.

Always back up any computer work on an external hard drive or a memory stick. Consider printing it off too. It is vital that you keep backup copies of what you are doing; if you don't, and your computer decides to take a break, you could lose weeks of work, if not more.

Organise your workstation. Keep your computer desktop tidy in the same way that you keep your physical desktop tidy. Clear out the clutter and aim for a clean, clear space in which to work. Practise the art of feng shui: clear out the physical and mental clutter and aim for a poised, efficient approach to your life and work.

Keep track of your information sources. Label any texts you download from the Internet and always record the details of books or articles you read. If you give a direct quotation, remember to give the page number. It is virtually impossible to retrieve a page number from a book, especially if it is back in the library.

Working with others

Remember that you have a life outside study, and friends and family who care about you. Pay attention to them and spend time with them. Negotiate with them that they will allow you time and space to write, and promise them that their reward will be to see you graduate.

Pay attention to your supervisor, too. They want you to succeed, and most supervisors put in far more effort than is ever recognised, so be nice to them and thank them for what they do. Behave in a professional way in relation to your work. Submit assignments by the due date and don't ask for extensions unless absolutely necessary. Aim to produce a clean, error-free, attractive text and always say thank you to those who deserve it.

Example 23

Many practitioners offer accounts of their collaborative action enquiries, and none more so than Joseph Shosh of Moravian College, Bethlehem, Pennsylvania. He writes about the collaborating institutions in North America, of which he and I and many mutual colleagues are members:

> The Action Research Network of the Americas (ARNA), the Collaborative Action Research Network (CARN), the Value and Virtue in Practice-Based Conference and network, and the Moravian Action Research Conference provide invaluable spaces within which practitioners may share the results of their inquiry. Recognizing and acting upon the 2012 motto 'To Know Is Not Enough', the American Educational Research Association's Action Research Special Interest Group has been instrumental in supporting ARNA's vision of developing a network of action research spaces throughout the western hemisphere to contribute to crucial worldwide efforts to empower practitioners to research their own practice. Following the lead of Margaret Riel's M.A. in Educational Technology Program at Pepperdine University, Moravian will endeavor to make its own action research conference sessions electronically available to action researchers around the world.
>
> (Shosh, 2013: 118–19)

You can also see online resources created by Margaret Riel at www.wikispaces.com. They are free to download and use as you wish.

Similarly, pay attention to work colleagues or other course members. Aim to set up critical friendships where you will comment on one another's work and give critical feedback. Use emails and social networking to share ideas and resources. Never take colleagues for granted, and be ready to volunteer to help them out too. You are all in this together, and working together helps everyone to succeed (as shown in Example 23).

We now turn to the business of producing your text.

PRODUCING YOUR TEXT

Before you begin writing your text, think about matters of communication, as outlined in Chapter 4. Remember that, when you write your text, you think of two aspects: telling the story and communicating the story. When you tell the story, you think of the content and form of your text; when you communicate it, you think of the best way to communicate the message to your reader.

Table 6.3 Questions to ask yourself when writing your text for a reader

Question	Possible response
What do I want to say? What is the topic or focus of my text?	Being clear about what you wish to say will keep you on track. Decide in advance what your topic is and stick to it throughout the text. This provides the 'golden thread' that runs right through your text
Who do I want to say it to? Who is my audience?	Have a sense of who you are writing for. Decide well in advance who your potential audience is, so that you can achieve the right tone and attitude for your writing
Why do I want to say it? What is important about what I am saying?	You have something special to say, and only you know what it is. Decide what is important about what you are saying, so that you can say it clearly and unambiguously. Have confidence in your knowledge. No one else has thought this before: you are making a contribution to knowledge of the field; your contribution could be seen as original. Be proud of what you are saying and speak with the confidence and authority that show you know what you are talking about
How am I going to say it? What will be the content and form of my text? How will I write it?	Depending on your audience, decide on the content and form of your text. Knowing who you are writing for will also help you to develop an appropriate tone and voice. Decide in advance how you are going to write it, whether as straight prose, or with lots of examples. Think about how you are going to tell the story of your research and what narrative style you are going to adopt
Why should people listen to me? What will people learn from what I am saying?	Think carefully about what is special about your work. Why should people listen to you? They are busy; why should they give you their time? What is in it for them? What will they get out of reading your text? How are you going to communicate this to your intended audience? Remember AIDA (attention, interest, desire, action)!
What is new about what I am saying? How does my research contribute to new thinking and new practices? How do I relate it to what other people have said about the topic in the past?	Yes, what *is* new about what you are saying? Do you make any new points? What are they? Be sure to spell these out to your reader, otherwise they may switch off or read someone else's work. It is your job as the author to spell out these things for your reader. Tell them what you are going to say, say it, and then tell them what you have said. Especially tell them what is special about what they are reading and why they should feel delighted that they have read it. Also point out that your ideas are a significant advance on what has been said about the topic previously

Table 6.3 continued

Question	Possible response
Where do I find this information? The literatures? The Internet? Other people?	This is where you do your background reading. You find out as much as you can about the topic you are studying. Explain this to your reader: tell them what authors you consulted; why those and not others; what was special about what you found out. Did your reading corroborate what you are saying, or are you saying something new and challenging and developing a new train of thought in the literatures?
How do I ensure the factual accuracy of my text? Where do I check my facts?	Be sure to be accurate. Do not write anything about which you have doubts. If you are expressing an opinion, say so, and don't try to pass off your opinion as fact. This means avoiding absolutist terms such as 'Surely . . .' and 'It is obvious that . . .'. Hold your thinking lightly and never make assumptions about something without checking the facts of the matter first
How do I ensure the technical accuracy of my report? How many times do I proofread? How do I get my references right?	Proofread multiple times. Make sure that every word is spelled correctly, every work cited in the text appears in the list of references and every sentence is grammatical and hangs together. Check your references multiple times. Do not depend on anyone else to do these things for you: there is no one else, and, even if there were, it is your job to take responsibility for your own work
How do I ensure the ethical accuracy of my report? Have I checked with everyone concerned before and after writing?	This is paramount. Check that you have included all letters requesting and granting permission to do the research. Check that you have included as appendices blank copies of all questionnaires, surveys, minutes of meetings, logs and diaries – anything that would count as evidence that your reader may wish to see, especially if the reader is an examiner

What kinds of question do you need to ask?

Table 6.3 shows some of the main questions you need to ask and some of the things you need to think about: there are many other general questions and points and some that are specific to your context. Aim to identify these and draw up a chart like the one in Table 6.3 to guide your thinking.

Now, think about how you will manage the writing process and what you need to do to make it accessible to your reader, so that your reader will see immediately what you are getting at and appreciate the value of what you have done and written.

Managing the writing process

It is generally agreed that producing a text takes the form of three stages: (1) planning, (2) composing and (3) editing and revising. Each one is as important as the others. Here is what they involve.

Planning

This involves all the aspects spoken about so far in this chapter. You need to think about the practical and financial feasibility of all aspects of the writing process, and you need also to think about what you wish to write, how you will write it and how you will hold your reader's attention throughout. Think also about what is special about your work that readers will admire and find useful for their own learning. Aim to plan your workload and the allocation of time and other resources. Think about how you are going to organise your material and how to manage its storage and retrieval. Think also how you will keep a record of all this.

Composing

Composing refers to the actual writing of the text. It is an action–reflection process that involves drafting, reading and revising, redrafting, re-reading and re-revising, until you are reasonably satisfied that you are saying what you wish to. Writers seldom achieve their best draft at the first try. More realistically, they go through multiple drafts, refining and re-refining. Sometimes, new writers think they will get there in one go, which is most unlikely.

Editing and revising

This stage is when you consider the text you have composed and begin to tidy it up. Editing happens at different levels. You can do light editing as you go, such as checking spelling and grammar and considering your choice of words and phrases. More serious editing happens when you have produced a draft and begin to look at it critically. This is when you begin to consider the text at the level of sentences and paragraphs. Revising is more extensive, when you begin considering a stretch of text, as in a chapter or even across chapters, and see if the text hangs together properly. Sometimes it does not, so you need to change it.

Revising is a focused and disciplined activity where you ask yourself questions that deserve an absolutely honest answer. An action plan for revising involves the following:

- Read the text through and revisit the question about who you are writing for and what you wish to say.

- Read through again, and ask: am I writing for my intended reader? Am I writing in a style and language that they will understand? Does the text flow easily?

If your answer is 'no' to any of these questions, ask yourself what you need to do to make things easier for your reader. You may decide to make changes at the level of words, sentences or paragraphs. Revisions at this local level could be achieved through using different words, writing in shorter sentences and checking that paragraphs hang together, putting text into boxes or bulleted lists, or inserting additional section headings to guide navigation. Revisions at a wider level may involve cutting and pasting larger chunks of text, rewriting sections or deleting material that turns out to be repetition of earlier points or even is now irrelevant.

Many writers spend hours and even days working on a small piece of text. It is useful, if you can, to read your text today and leave it overnight or for a few days before revisiting it and reading it again. Perceptions change in interims. Keep reading your text as much as possible, but also be aware that you will probably never get it right to your entire satisfaction.

Polishing

This is a nice stage, when you polish up your text. You may spend a lot of time on a word or phrase, depending on how much time you have. I tend to polish a lot; I am fussy about the sound of a sentence and finding the right word, and I like to turn in a professional-looking text to the publisher. Besides, the more finished the text is at manuscript stage, the less work the production team has to do, and the quicker it gets to publication. So, it is worthwhile spending time and effort in the last stages of polishing.

Proofreading

Learn how to proofread: it is a practice that will last you for life. Proofreading means checking every word in the text to see if any errors are still present. Different strategies are recommended in the literatures. You can read the text out loud or listen to the voice in your head as it reads the text out loud. If you really want to do a thorough job, go through the text word by word and mark off each word as you read it. Aim to proofread your entire text at least three times while you are producing it. Do a final proofread before you submit it. Being conscientious about what your work looks like is a sign of professionalism and good practice.

Learn to listen to yourself

An aspect of proofreading is to listen to yourself as you write. It is a core aspect of writing, too, when you hear the words in your head and write them down – a kind of dictation to the self. When you proofread, you read the text back to yourself. This acts as a double bonus, because you also re-hear the music of the text. You listen to the cadence and check whether it sounds right. If a sentence or a word does not sound right, take this as a sign that it needs changing, and change it. Do not let anything go to your reader that you are not happy with yourself.

Summary

This chapter has considered ideas about learning to produce a text, which involves learning about the writing process itself. It has looked at two issues in particular: first, getting ready to write, where it offers advice about gathering ideas, organising yourself, understanding your own habits and routines, staying healthy and organising your time; and second, producing a text, working with others and managing the writing process, including planning, composing, editing and revising and polishing. Ideas are offered throughout about how to do these things, with the aim of producing a high-quality text.

A key part of producing a text is knowing how to structure your text. This becomes the focus of Chapter 7, where we consider the different kinds of structure you can use for writing up your action research project.

Chapter 7

How do I write an action research report or master's dissertation?

This chapter is about how to write an action research report or dissertation. It suggests some possible outline structures and gives advice on the most important things that should appear in the text. Chapter 8 explains how your project report or dissertation is judged.

The chapter contains these sections:

- Possible structures for writing your dissertation;
- What goes into different sections.

Knowing how to write up your action research project is especially important these days, with increasing interest in the certification of professional learning. Many professions insist on workplace-based training for internal or external accreditation. You are expected to demonstrate knowledge of practices, contexts, literatures and research, as well as capacity in writing. Your report should show the achievement of academic criteria, as well as quality in practice, research and communication.

POSSIBLE STRUCTURES FOR WRITING YOUR DISSERTATION

This section outlines some possible structures for organising your text. Although an action research text can be flexible, there does need to be an obvious and easily navigable structure, so that your reader can locate themselves in the text.

Before looking at possible structures for an action research report, check that you are clear about the structures of the conventional social science reports that many higher education institutions still expect. Always check what your accrediting institution is looking for and write your action research report accordingly.

Three possible outline structures for producing a report are presented here. Which one you choose depends on what your institution requires and what you and your supervisor decide will be best for you. The three outline structures are:

1 a standard structure for a social sciences report;
2 a standard structure for a social sciences report within which you can adapt your action research report;
3 a narrative action research structure.

A standard structure for a social sciences report

A standard social sciences report is written using specific section headings, as set out below. Most higher education institutions expect this kind of structure, and you would be expected to use it if you are in a traditionalist institution. The same structure is also used for submissions to the more established, often corporate-oriented research conferences. You can find many examples in most research methodologies books and in many online institutional guidelines. The structure of a conventional social science report looks something like this:

- Abstract
- Introduction
- Aims and objectives
- Literature review
- Methodology
- Findings/results
- Discussion
- Conclusion
- References.

Table 7.1 on page 130 shows what is usually written in the different sections of this kind of report.

What are the expectations for this kind of report?

The expectations for this kind of conventional social sciences report are as follows:

- You present everything in an objective way. The values that inspired the research are not considered.
- Your language is to the point.
- The report is written in the third person: the first person 'I' seldom appears.
- The passive voice tends to be used a lot.
- There is little personal reflection. There is no supposition.
- The work is presented as if you always knew what you know now. The development of personal thinking does not appear, and there is no reflection on personal learning.

Table 7.1 Contents of a conventional social science report

Section	Contents
Abstract	A brief overview of the research project, including research aims, question, rationale, methodology, findings and significance for knowledge of the field. The abstract for a dissertation should be not more than a single page
Introduction	General introduction to the research and its contexts, aims and objectives; claim to knowledge stated; main contexts; overview of research and findings. The report follows a systematic argument and focuses on demonstrating a conclusive outcome
Aims and objectives	Research issue and rationale. Reasons are given for doing the research, usually communicated in terms of demonstrating a cause-and-effect relationship. Articulate your research question. This often takes the form of an assertion that can be supported with evidence, e.g. 'An investigation into the relationship between x and y'. The report follows a systematic argument and focuses on demonstrating a conclusive outcome
Literature review	Engage with relevant substantive and methodology literatures, usually chosen to show support for the argument you are making, though engagement with counter-arguments is acceptable. Literatures are well organised. There is little discussion of problematics. There is an expectation that your literatures will support what you are saying and provide additional evidence for the conclusions you have reached
Methodology	The story is told in a systematic way, leading towards a definitive conclusion. There is an outline of main events in the research story. Ideas are presented in a neat and tidy way. Your story tends to adopt a one-dimensional format and time sequence (no backstory, no flashbacks, no reflections from the past). You do not focus on developments in your own thinking, only on the topic you are investigating. Consideration for ethical issues is clarified
Findings	Say what you have found out, in an objective way. Avoid talking about the confusion or difficulties of finding out
Discussion	Discuss some of the main issues arising from the research and match what you have found with what other people have found, also as communicated through the literatures
Conclusion	Summarise everything and locate your findings in a context. You may note some limitations of your work and make suggestions about how it could have been done differently

Here are two examples from the literatures about how you could organise your text. Phillips and Pugh write:

Introduction (including aims);
Literature survey (background theory as a review of the relevant literature);
Method (data theory including a description of what has been done);
Results (focal theory including what was found);
Discussion (development of focal theory and suggestions for future work);
Conclusions (summary and contribution).

(Phillips and Pugh, 2005: 60)

Murray recommends a generic structure, as follows:

Generic thesis structure

- **Introduction/Background/Review of literature**
  Summarize and evaluate books, articles, theses, etc.
  Define the gap in the literature
  Define and justify your project
- **Theory/Approach/Method/Materials/Subject**
  Define method, theoretical approach, instrument
  Method of inquiry
  Show links between your method and others
  Justify your method
- **Analysis/Results**
  Report what you did, list steps followed
  Document the analysis, showing how you carried it out
  Report what you found
  Prioritize sections for the thesis or for an appendix
- **Interpretation/Discussion**
  Interpret what you found
  Justify your interpretation
  Synthesize results in illustrations, tables, graphs, etc.
- **Conclusion/Implications/Recommendations**
  For future research
  For future practice
  Report issues which were beyond the scope of this study

(Murray, 2002: 116–17)

The issue now arises that, if you are doing an action research project in an institution that expects this kind of social sciences structure, you need to find a way to adapt your story to the existing structures. This need not be as difficult as it sounds. Here are some ideas about how you can do it.

A standard social science structure within which you can adapt an action research report

The following shows how you can fit an action research story into a social sciences outline structure, with the main points you would need to put into the different sections. In the third outline structure, on page 136, these points are expanded and supplemented with further ideas.

Box 7.1 Fitting an action research report into a standard social science structure

Abstract

The abstract is a brief overview of the research project, including research aims, question, rationale, methodology, findings and its significance for knowledge of the field. For a dissertation, it should not be more than a single page.

Introduction

The introduction should contain the following:

- a general introduction to the research and its contexts, aims and objectives, main achievements and findings;
- a stated claim to knowledge; a statement of what you have learned through doing the research, about yourself and other aspects;
- the main contexts: social (local or wider setting); professional or organisational (what is happening in your institution?); policy (what do the literatures say?); historical (what is the general/your specific history?); other?
- an overview of research and main findings: what you have found out about: (a) the topic you are studying, (b) yourself and your learning, (c) other people, (d) systems and other people's views and behaviours, and (e) anything else;
- an acknowledgement that the research (and report) shows systematic progression and comes to provisional conclusions, without necessarily reaching a conclusive outcome; acknowledgement of progress in learning as well as development of actions taken.

Aims and objectives

- The aim of the report is to give an account of the research you have been doing. The aim of the research was to discover knowledge (learn) or create new knowledge (learn new things) about how you

---

have improved the quality of your practices and learning in collaboration with others. Creating new knowledge of practice and explaining how you have done so amount to generating your own theory of practice.

- Say what you hoped to achieve through doing your research.
- Spell out your research issue (what you wanted to find out) and your claim to knowledge (what you have found out).
- Articulate your research question. This can often take the form, 'How do I improve what I am doing?' – for example, 'How do I understand my management practices better?' Explain that this is grounded in your values.
- Frame your report as identifying an issue in your workplace that you wished to investigate and explain that you will test the validity of your claim to knowledge through the work. Your report follows a systematic argument and focuses on demonstrating how the situation you are investigating has improved (or not) and the processes of your own and other people's learning.

Rationale

- Give reasons and purposes for doing the research. Reasons are usually written as explaining how you are trying to live your values in your practices in relation to others in different contexts. Purposes are usually written as saying how you hope to contribute to new understandings and practices that will make life better for all: this has to be negotiated in relation to other people's perspectives.
- Explain how you have negotiated your values with other people. You have not imposed anything on others.
- Explain how your research is intended to contribute to other people's understandings and practices: for example, a possible contribution to new organisational relationships or new policy formation and implementation.

Literature review

- You may or may not do a chapter that stands as a literature review. If not, you engage with the literatures throughout, possibly as mini-reviews within different chapters: for example, you could do a review of methodology issues in a methodology chapter.
- The literatures are chosen in relation to the subject area of your research (nursing, carpentry, landscape gardening) and your methodology (action research, narrative enquiry, mixed methodologies) or any other frameworks, as appropriate to your research.
- Discuss your research in light of what the literatures say. Draw on concepts in the literatures to help you frame your research: these

become your conceptual frameworks (think of a framework as a scaffolding or armature, like the ones that sculptors use, around which to construct their sculpture).

- You may agree or disagree with the literatures. If you disagree, you should come up with your own ideas and not leave an empty conceptual space.
- If appropriate, you can use the literatures to provide additional evidence, or counter-evidence, for the conclusions you have reached.
- You adopt throughout a critical approach where you problematise both what the literatures say and your own thinking. You explain that you are open to modifying your ideas in light of better arguments.
- Approach the literatures in a conversational mode. Imagine that the authors are speaking with you, sharing their ideas, and you are invited into that conversation as a valuable contributor.
- You can also access the literatures online, using video resources and tutorials, YouTube, audio and e-books and websites. You can develop your own website and blog to show how you are engaging with other people's ideas and negotiating or adapting their ideas to your own.
- Use social media such as Twitter or Facebook to share ideas and access new ones.

Methodology

- Give all the details of how you organised your research. Say what methodology you used (action research, narrative enquiry, mixed methodologies); why you used this one and not another; and what might have been some of the problematics involved.
- Explain who your participants were and why you chose them.
- Explain how you considered all ethical aspects and submitted your ethics statement to your institutional ethics committee for approval. Include your original request and permissions letter from the ethics committee as an appendix to your report.
- Tell the story as it happened, leading towards the point where you came to a conclusion, or not; you may find that there is no definitive conclusion to your enquiry.
- Tell two parallel stories: the story of what happened in the social/ organisational world and the story of your learning. The story of your learning may appear as learning with and from others.
- Present emergent findings as new knowledge. Include the possible untidiness of the experience to show the complexity of the situation you were in. Your story could adopt a linear format and also could include a backstory, flashbacks and reflections from the past. Show

developments in your own thinking and in your understanding of the topic you are investigating.

- Also show, if appropriate, how you influenced other people's thinking, and how they, in turn, took action within their personal and social situations.
- Include information about how you gathered data, identified and chose criteria, adopted specific analytical techniques, coded and sorted the data, generated evidence and tested its authenticity against the critical feedback of others. Say whether you kept a research journal and whether this was useful.
- Say how you set up triangulation techniques, consulted with others such as critical friends, convened validation groups and negotiated feedback.

Findings

- Say what you have found out, both about your topic and about yourself.
- Also talk, if appropriate, about how you have influenced others to investigate their practices too: this idea of 'impact' becomes a key criterion.
- Where appropriate, talk about the confusion or difficulties of learning. Talk about any other matter that has had particular significance for you through doing the research.

Discussion

- Discuss some of the main issues arising from the research and match what you have found with what other people have found, as communicated through the literatures.
- Explain how your learning is helping other people also to conduct similar investigations into their practices.
- Say whether you think your research has been successful and in whose terms. Give possible reasons why it has been successful, or why not.
- Say why the learning from this research has been valuable for yourself, especially in terms of how you have generated your own theory of practice.

Conclusion

- Summarise everything and locate your findings in a context.
- Note any limitations of your work and make suggestions about how it could have been done differently. Say how you might do things differently in future.
- Suggest new directions for future research: show how this cycle of action research transforms into the next cycle.

What are the expectations of this kind of report?

The expectations for this kind of action research report are as follows:

- You present everything from your own point of view. The values that inspired the research provide the starting point for the research.
- Your language is to the point, but also includes pieces of reflective writing.
- The report is written in the first person: the first person 'I' tells the story, recognising that the 'I' is always in company with other 'I's. The research report uses a narrative form.
- You use the active voice throughout.
- There is a good deal of personal reflection. Conclusions are held lightly and open to revision.
- The work is presented as a story of learning. The development of personal thinking appears as part of the story: in some cases, it becomes the central theme of the story.
- Nothing is taken for granted. You hold everything open to interrogation. However, you balance your open stance with an explicitly articulated commitment to try to live in the direction of your values, and also to be open to others' values too.
- You show throughout respect for others' positions, opinions and cultural sensitivities and position yourself as a participant with them in a wider life project.

Now look at the third kind of structure.

A narrative action research structure

If you are in an institution that accepts action research, you can use a different structure and form of language for your report. Now, you adopt a full narrative form and adapt your section headings to reflect the process of an action enquiry.

Before you begin, you may find it useful to revisit the core principles of action research by working through an action enquiry, as in Table 7.2, and use this as a conceptual basis for writing your report.

The answers you give on your worksheet will generate a story that adapts to the following set of points and questions:

- Introduction.
- Context.
- What did I wish to investigate? What was my concern? What did I hope to find out?
- Why did I want to investigate this area? Why was this a concern? What are my contexts?
- How could I show the situation as it was? How did I monitor practices and gather data?

Table 7.2 Working through an action enquiry

Issue / question	Response
What really matters to me? What do I care passionately about? What kind of difference do I want to make in the world?	
What are my values, and why do I hold them?	
What am I interested in investigating? What is the research issue? What is my research question?	
Why do I wish to investigate this particular issue?	
What data can I gather to show the situation as it is (my contexts, current thinking) and the reasons for my concerns?	
What can I do about it? What are my options?	
What will I do about it? How will I do it? When will I do it? Who will I ask to help me? Why those people and not others? What resources will I need?	
What kind of evidence will I produce from the data to show the situation as it unfolds? How will I decide which pieces of data are relevant? Which criteria will I use?	
How will I ensure that any conclusions I come to are reasonably fair and accurate? How do I test the validity of my provisional claims to knowledge? Who will I involve in validation meetings? Why those people and not others?	
How will I modify my concerns, ideas and actions in light of my evaluation?	
How will I explain the significance of my action research? Who is the research significant? Who says?	

- What could I do about it?
- What did I do about it? How did I do it?
- How did I continue to monitor practices and gather data?
- How did I analyse and interpret my data in order to generate evidence? What was the importance of doing so?
- How did I arrive at some preliminary conclusions?
- How did I test the validity of these conclusions and my claim to knowledge?
- How did I modify my practices in light of my evaluation?
- What is the potential significance of what I have done?

If you bring your answers to the business of writing your report, you can structure the report according to the following sections.

WHAT GOES INTO DIFFERENT SECTIONS

Abstract

This gives a summary of the work, including research aims, question, rationale, methodology, findings and potential significance for knowledge of the field. The length of the abstract will depend on the length of the assignment. The abstract should summarise the main features of the research, including the knowledge claim and a clear outline of how the validity of the claim has been tested throughout the work. It is usually reckoned that an abstract for a master's dissertation should be between 250 and 400 words in length; it should be no more than a single page.

Example 24

Here is an example of an abstract for a Master's in Education dissertation, from Marian Nugent (2000).

This study shows, I believe, an improvement in my teaching of the Junior Certificate Schools Programme (JCSP) students. The philosophy of the JCSP is that every student is capable of success. It describes the shift in my thinking and practice from a view of reality as objectified to a view of reality as holistic and integrated. Carr and Kemmis (1986: 24) state: 'A humanistic perspective emphasises that education is a human encounter whose aim is the development of the unique potential of each individual.'

I believe my practice demonstrates this quality. The question that informed my research was: 'How can I raise the level of self-esteem of second year JCSP students and create a better learning environment?' I set out to explore this question in a number of ways: in terms of my own professional development as a reflective practitioner and in terms of the students' development.

In my work with the students I have attempted to develop their respect for one another, to managing behaviour and classroom discipline. I have fostered a climate of mutual respect between the students and myself as year head. The research was in the overall context of classroom management and I followed an action research methodology to locate my research.

A problem which I encountered was that as an authority figure it is easy to maintain the status quo but it is difficult to imagine how things could be different. I have implemented practices, which can be used in order to show a move to a different style of discipline, to teaching and care for the students.

Action research aims to improve our practice and our understanding of that practice. For me, my educational journey has evolved as a result of participation on the MA in Education programme and I am now further towards my goals of being more understanding of the students and their needs, and of encouraging students to believe in their own powers of learning.

(Nugent, 2000)

Introduction

Your introduction provides a general introduction to your research and its context. It engages with the questions: 'What did I wish to investigate? What was my concern?'

Spell out your research issue and your claim to knowledge, that is, what you know now that you did not know before. Articulate your research question, using the form, 'How do I improve what I am / we are doing?' – for example, 'How do I understand my management practices better?' or 'How do we help patients to develop an enhanced sense of independence?' Frame your report as identifying an issue in your workplace that you wished to investigate and explain that you will test the validity of your claim to knowledge through the work. Outline briefly how you have tried to live your values and how this idea frames your research: these include your ontological, epistemological, methodological, practical and sociocultural values. Your report follows a systematic argument and focuses on demonstrating how the situation you are investigating has improved (or not) and the processes of your own and other people's learning. Explain how your report can stand as your personal theory of practice. Outline your methodology and how this is communicated through the chapters of your report, and explain how this also shows the methodological features of action research.

Begin by asking this question:

What did I wish to investigate? What was my concern? What did I hope to find out?

Say what your research interest was and the situation you wished to investigate. The term 'a social situation' always refers to people together. What was your situation with others, such that you wanted to investigate it? (see Examples 25 and 26, on page 140).

Example 25

Lāsma Latsone and Linda Pavitola (2013) provide an introduction to their research as follows:

> Citizenship and civic responsibility are topical issues in educational programmes in Latvia, but their core principles tend not always to be lived in people's lives. There is a lot of passive learning in this regard, and civic knowledge often remains at a theoretical level without becoming a value for the everyday life of citizens, including, in the context of education, students.
>
> In Latvian society everyday understanding of civic responsibility has been greatly influenced by historical events and national culture; the same can be said about the notion of what it means to be part of a community. Working with emerging teachers and discussing different issues in Intercultural Education and Cultural Heritage in Education classes, we authors have observed that many students lack a critical understanding about civic matters and that they tend to associate civic responsibility with patriotism and the preservation of national and cultural values, neglecting the communal aspect necessary for purposeful action and involvement.
>
> In this chapter we consider the following issues:
>
> • Is community a lived value for our students, and how much are they prepared to take action for the benefit of the larger community?
> • Do we, as adults and teachers, set a good example for our students?
> • How can higher education contribute to educating students for civic responsibility and help them to transform this value into a virtue?
>
> (Latsone and Pavitola, 2013: 93)

Example 26

A second example is from the introduction to a book chapter by Paul Murphy (2000), adapted from his master's dissertation, that sets the scene for the research.

> My work is to do with the rehabilitation of sexual offenders in religious communities. A member of a religious community myself, I work in a counselling role both with offenders and also with the members of the communities into which they will become reintegrated. My work is educational in its broadest sense, in that I am trying to help all members of the community to find tolerant and compassionate ways of living with

one another in the face of personal and collective distress. I have to help all members of the community learn how to cope with new, traumatic circumstances . . . To help me draw up some provisional guidelines [about learning to cope] I decided to enroll on the MA in Education course, in the hope that I would have the opportunity to investigate my practice to help me understand better the nature of what I was doing.

(Murphy, 2000: 154; the story continues below)

Contexts

Set out what your contexts are. They could include the following:

- Your professional context: whether you are an engineer, a tree surgeon or a plumber, and where you work. Do not give the name of your workplace unless you have written permission to do so (see the section on ethics in Chapter 8).
- Your social context: are you a member of a club or a manager? Does your social context provide an important aspect of your work, perhaps in the community?
- Your personal context: are you disadvantaged in any way? Do you work from home? Is your research about family life?
- Your historical context: is your research influenced by your own history? Perhaps you were in a particular kind of school where you learned specific social and cultural stories. Talk about how these experiences give a particular context to your current research. Events that happened in the past may also act as impulses for your current research interests, as in Example 27.

Example 27

Here is an extract from the master's dissertation of Zola Malgas, who works as a school principal in Khayelitsha, South Africa.

My Personal Background

I was born and grew up at Mdantsane, a township in the Eastern Cape, South Africa. Eastern Cape is rated amongst the poorest provinces in South Africa. When I was two years old my parents divorced and my mother had to look for a job. She took us to my grandmother who lived in a rural area. I started schooling there in a mission school, which was constituted of ten classrooms enrolling grades one to seven. These classrooms were made of mud. I hated schooling there. The distance we travelled to and from school was more than fifteen kilometres and most of the time we went to school bare-footed irrespective of the season of the year. I still remember being unable to cross the river when it was raining. I used to cry a lot, I still have dreadful memories, and the thought still terrifies me even today. I was not interested in learning at all because I did not have any reason for going to school. Nobody ever told me the purpose of schooling.

When I was in grade one, on one occasion I did not go to school for five days, for no reason, without anyone noticing. When my mother was told about it, she punished me severely and the following day she went to school to report to my teachers that I had not had any reason for being absent from school. She told them the whole story about her family history. My school principal gave me a good spanking, so much so that I was unable to sit at my desk afterwards. One good thing about the experience of that day was that I was told the purpose of schooling for the first time in my entire life. My principal told me that the only way I could get out of the misery we were experiencing at home was to become educated so that I would not find myself in the same position my mother was in when I grew up. Everything she said made sense to me and from that day onwards I was never absent from school. . . .

It is from this background that I find myself obliged to explain the rationale behind my work as an educator, before I even speak about teaching learners any algebra or geometry.

(Malgas, 2009)

Why did I want to investigate this area? Why was this a concern?

Say why it was important for you to investigate this area. Did it impinge on you personally? Was it a case that your values were being denied, perhaps through institutional influences? Give reasons and purposes for doing the research, explaining how you are trying to live your values in your practices in relation to others in sociopolitical, cultural, personal and organisational contexts.

As an extension of your contexts or background chapters, you may or may not do a chapter that stands as a literature review of a specific area, such as dementia or learning styles (see the advice offered in Chapter 4) (see also Example 28 on page 143).

How could I show the situation as it was? How did I monitor practices and gather data?

At this point, say how you monitored practice and gathered data. Be clear about whose practices you are monitoring. In McNiff (2016), I outline four important and interrelated sources of data: your learning, your actions, other

Example 28

Here is an account by Bente Norbe, Odd Edvardsen and Anne-Lise Thoresen, who work as professional educators in nursing and healthcare at UiT The Arctic University in North Norway. They write (2013: 69):

> In 2009, the University College in Tromsø and the University of Tromsø applied for permission to merge into one institution, as a national pilot, and reorganised with new faculties and new departments. Before the merger, colleagues in the newly created Faculty of Health Sciences and in the Department of Health and Care Sciences had been located in the university and the university college, and therefore had different identities, responsibilities and self-perceptions. Traditionally, research in our department has been restricted to only a few researchers working within specialised fields. Little or no research has been conducted in the field of health care education and educational practices.
>
> We three all have considerable experience in the practice field. Odd and Bente have been involved in nursing education for more than twenty years, and Anne-Lise in the midwifery programme for fifteen years. However, research has not been a priority for us as professional educators, and we have until now tended to see research as the province of other researchers – their research – something distant from us because of our key focus on teaching and education. Added to this has been the generally low expectation that professional educators should develop capacity in research, with a lack of adequate funding to support any efforts in this regard.
>
> However, a requirement in the newly formed departments in the faculty was to develop research groups and increase research capacity. We as a group broadened this view to see educational practice as a form of research in itself. This has been challenging and has required us to develop new perceptions of ourselves as both professional educators and researchers.
>
> Norbye *et al.* (2013: 70)

people's learning and other people's actions. All are in a mutually reciprocal and transformational relationship, as in Figure 7.1 on page 144: your learning influences your actions, which have the potential to influence other people's learning, and this influences their actions. Equally, their learning and actions can influence yours.

Explain also how you gathered the data and why you chose those particular data-gathering methods. For example, Josephine Bleach (2013: 24–5)

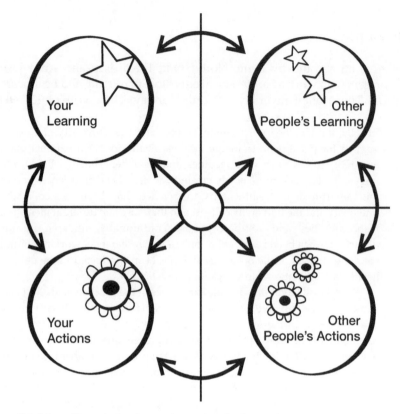

Figure 7.1 Mutually reciprocal transformational relationships

outlines ways in which she and her colleagues used questionnaires, observations, documentary data, interviews and assessment of and for learning in the form of standardised test results (see also www.september books.com/valueandvirtue.asp). Participant Nikki (in Walker and Solvason, 2014) outlined how she collected data, as follows:

> The first method of data collection was questionnaires. . . . The design used open and closed questions. Using open ended questions gives participants the opportunity to fully express themselves in their own manner. Whilst closed questions would elicit either a yes or no answer . . . The next method of collecting data was to conduct interviews. I decided I would carry out two types, one to one interviews and a mini-focus group. These would be useful as they would follow up the questionnaires.
>
> (Walker and Solvason, 2014: 78, 80)

A point to note: make sure your data are relevant to your research question. It is easy to collect data willy-nilly and find that little is really useful. It is important to identify working criteria for making judgements about the relevance of the data, so that you will be able to transform the data into evidence in due course.

Methodology

Tell the story as it happened, leading towards the point where you came to a conclusion – or not: you may find that there is no definitive conclusion to your enquiry. You tell two parallel stories: the story of what happened in the social world and the story of your learning. The story of your learning may appear as learning with and from others. You present emergent findings as new knowledge if appropriate. Speak about the untidy nature of the experience to show the complexity of the situation you were in. Your story adopts a non-linear format that can include the backstory, flashbacks and reflections from the past. You show developments in your own thinking and in your understanding of the topic you are investigating. You also show, if appropriate, how you influenced other people's thinking and how they, in turn, took action within their personal and social situations.

Example 29

Here is the continuation of Paul Murphy's story:

> It was here that I came to study research methods. I studied empirical, interpretive and critical methodologies; and I decided to investigate my practice using an action research methodology. This, I felt, would enable me to research my own practice and generate my own theory of how I could help offenders and their communities. The attractions of the action research approach were that it required me to study my own work, that it did not expect answers but invited further questions, and acknowledged what Schön (1983) refers to as the 'messiness' of real life. I related strongly to all these qualities in what I was doing, and was glad to have found a methodology that paralleled and legitimated the complex and developmental form of my work.
>
> (Murphy, 2000: 154; the full story may be found in McNiff, 2000)

What could I do about it?

Say how at this point you considered your options for action. This was a political decision, because taking action tends to be about trying to influence processes of personal and social change. It can mean, for example, turning your values into action. A powerful conceptual framework for this idea is offered by Argyris and Schön (1978). They explain how we all hold espoused theories (what we like to think we do), and yet these are not always the same as our theories in use (what we actually do). The task for practitioners is how to reconcile the two, as in Example 30.

Example 30

Ray O'Neill (2006), in Ireland, explains how he helps young people to learn how to take political action by taking control of their vocational learning. He shows a videotape of students working together and analyses their actions as follows:

> The students are taking action to change their own circumstances by developing their own capacity for action through communication. The students are talking together and working together to achieve inter-subjective communication with a view to taking political action; political action in the form of taking control of their own lives.
>
> (O'Neill, 2006)

What did I do about it? How did I do it?

At this point, you say what you did in the practice domain. You continue to monitor the action and gather data about what you are doing. You can use the same data-gathering techniques as before, or you can use different ones. When you write up your action research, you also tell the story of how you hoped to influence processes of social change (see Example 31 on page 147).

Now, think about how you will analyse and interpret your data. You ask:

How did I analyse and interpret my data in order to generate evidence? What was the importance of doing so?

Remember that the methodology of your entire text aims to show the procedures for testing the validity of your knowledge claim. In the first instance, you gather data to show the initial stages of the claim as it begins to emerge; you then go on to a more rigorous, explanatory level when you turn the data into evidence. So, when you begin to analyse your data, it is important to identify criteria and standards that will help you make sense of them. Criteria are those things by which we make judgements: if you go shopping for a coat, you will make your decisions about which coat to buy based on the criteria of colour, size, fit, fashionableness and price. In making decisions about the validity of your claim, you identify your values as your criteria (see McNiff, 2016). Do you show how you live in the direction of your value of social justice? If you can produce data that show this to be the

Example 31

In a project conducted in 1993, Rita Fitzgerald and Sr Antoinette Keelan, both school principals in Ireland, outlined what they and staff did to improve the quality of staff meetings. They wrote:

> We decided to start our action research by investigating the present perceptions of our own staff members regarding aspects of school staff meetings. Questionnaires were distributed to staff members . . . and the responses collected and collated.
>
> The collated responses were then printed and distributed to staff members for on-going discussion. Meanwhile we ourselves had been inquiring into the negative influences prevailing, by comparing experiences and reviewing minutes of former meetings.
>
> Using the insights thus gleaned, and the positive attitudes engendered in the staff by the questionnaire exercise and consequent discussions, we then worked towards establishing a whole-staff consensus on what a staff meeting ought to be. We hope in this way to lead all the members to commit themselves to an ideal of collaboration and shared responsibility which will be reflected in the enhanced quality and effectiveness of our staff meetings.
>
> (Fitzgerald and Keelan, 1994: 184)

case, you can potentially turn those data into evidence. You select and take out of your data archive those data that meet your criteria and place them in a new evidence archive. You then test the authenticity of your evidence against the critical feedback of others.

You can also draw on methods such as triangulation to test for consistency among data and possibly among data-gathering methods. Bell says of the process of triangulation that it is a method to 'cross-check findings, and in a more extensive study, to use more than one method of data collecting' (2005: 116). She cites Laws *et al.* as saying:

> Accounts collected from different perspectives may not match tidily at all. There may be mismatch and even conflict between them. A mismatch does not necessarily mean that the data collection process is flawed – it could be that people just have very different accounts of similar phenomena. You need critically to examine the meaning of any mismatches to make sense of them.
>
> (Laws *et al.*, 2003: 281)

Triangulation is one method of testing the validity of conclusions. You also invite critical friends to comment on the way you conducted your research, the quality of your data and evidence. You invite a validation group to comment on the rigour of your methodology and the quality of your findings.

For example in Example 32, Mzuzile Mpondwana (2009) explains how he tested the validity of his knowledge claims against the critical feedback of colleagues. In doing so he engages with the following question:

How did I make sure that my conclusions I came to were reasonably fair and accurate?

Example 32

Mzuzile writes:

> I asked [colleagues] if they would like to come and observe me teaching in class. I wanted them to see that I was not trying to police them about how to deliver the curriculum in class but to see ways through which we could help each other improve our practice. I wanted to ease the anxieties of any of those educators who were still skeptical and nervous about engaging in the initiative. I wanted to create a culture of collaboration and working together for the main purpose of improving performance and the results in our department. I felt that everybody should feel free to express their views without reservation. The fact that the enthusiasm was there to enable educators to work towards achieving our goal as the department was a step in the right direction and a reason for rejoicing.
>
> I took my values as my living standards of judgement to assess the quality of my work and my research. Values are what give meaning to our lives: 'Every one of us lives according to values' (McNiff, 2002, p. 5). I value democracy: The fact that educators voluntarily agreed to study and reflect on their practices was what made me proud of my work. I value work that is productive and of the highest quality. The commitment made by my colleagues towards reflecting on and studying their practice is a recipe for all, a good foundation that would lead to the improvement of results. Seeing a group of educators sitting and reflecting on their practice in a more dialogical context was wonderful.
>
> (Mpondwana, 2009: 15)

How did I arrive at some preliminary conclusions?

At this point, you say what you have found out through doing your research, both about your topic and about yourself. You discuss some of the main issues arising from the research and match what you have found with what other people have found, as communicated through the literatures. You also discuss, if appropriate, how you have influenced others to investigate their practices too: this idea of 'impact' becomes a key criterion. Where appropriate, you talk about the confusion or difficulties of doing your research.

Example 33

Gill Bishop, Head of Programme, Postgraduate Business at York St John University, tells the story of her research journey in supporting full-time MBA students in their development to become critically reflective, reflexive practitioners. She says:

> Storytelling is widely acknowledged as a form of learning and as a way of understanding the cultures, customs and practices of the organisations in which we work (Boyce, 1996; Fawcett and Fawcett, 2011; Gold, Holman and Thorpe, 2002; Morgan and Dennehy, 1997). In this research, storytelling was adopted as a pedagogical approach and as an assessment process to support full time international postgraduate MBA students in developing the skills of reflection, critical reflection and reflexivity. Through a range of [data gathering techniques] to explore how students engaged in reflective practice (including questionnaires, observation and the use of focus groups), this led to a deeper questioning of my own practices in terms of reflective practice and whether I was meeting the requirements of a reflective practitioner appropriate for teaching the subject.
>
> One of the outcomes of my research was to question my own pedagogy in supporting MBA students to become reflective practitioners. This was partly supported when examining the value of verbal interaction as integral to the development of the skills of reflection (Collin and Karsenti, 2011; Cunliffe, 2002, 2004; Vygotsky, 1962). Reflexivity and the ability to learn from our experience is an essential skill required of managers today operating in a chaotic, complex and fast-changing global work environment. This led me to consider that over-reliance on more traditional classroom-based learning processes may fail to engage participants achieving in the deeper and more critical reflexive skills required of managers today.
>
> (Bishop, 2015)

How did I modify my practices in light of my evaluation?

At this point, you reflect on any changes that doing your action research has inspired. How have you developed your practices? Here is a powerful piece of writing from Sally Aston, a senior lecturer in design and technology, who writes about how she has come to a new place through doing her research.

Example 34

Sally says:

> By undertaking this research I have identified ways I can transform and improve my practice in future, as a practitioner reflecting in and on action. I believe that some [research] participants [now] have the opportunity to develop a deeper level of critical consciousness. I feel that if I encourage students to make closer connections with the natural environment and the wider global community, their level of critical engagement will be raised and they will feel that they, as participating and informed citizens, can change things for the better. At this time of transition we have reached what Freire described as an 'historical epoch', which is 'characterised by a series of aspirations, concerns and values in search of fulfilment' (2005: 4). As citizens, we can participate in these epochs by creating, recreating and making decisions which will influence our future. I think it is my responsibility in my position [as senior lecturer] to influence both future teachers and, indirectly, their pupils, to encourage participation as citizens who have the power to instigate positive change in society. . . . With this in mind, I want to continue to develop my learning of ways to improve and understand my practice, as a form of praxis ... where I feel I comfortably inhabit my values.
>
> (Aston, 2008: 22–3)

What is the potential significance of what I have done?

Chapter 9 contains ideas about the potential significance of what you have done in relation to the learning of yourself, of others and of your organisation. We return to the conversation then.

Summary

This chapter has looked at the possible structures you can use for writing an action research report or dissertation. It has first considered three possible structures you can use for writing your dissertation: a standard structure for a social sciences report, a standard structure for a social sciences report within which you can adapt your action research report, and a narrative action research structure. The chapter has then considered what goes into different sections, with worked examples.

We now turn to Part III, which is about how your work may be judged in terms of the content and form of your report, as well as the quality of your text. These matters are considered in some detail in the next chapter.

Part III

Reflecting and evaluating

Part III contains ideas about reflecting on what you have written and evaluating it in terms of whether it will meet required academic criteria, as well as fulfil expectations about the quality of content, form and communication. This is explored in Chapters 8–10.

Chapter 8 is about judging the quality of your text. It outlines internationally agreed requirements for work that qualifies for accreditation at different levels of difficulty. It also outlines how the quality of the action of action research is judged, as well as the quality of the research. Quality of writing is also considered. All these different aspects together amount to how you as a person are judged as a competent and capable practitioner and researcher.

Chapter 9 is about the potential significance of your work for different constituencies: for yourself, for others, including those in your organisation, and for the world. This aspect is part of the politics of action research, and of research in more general terms. It is suggested that, by producing your text, you can transform the existing knowledge base of academic writing into a new one that includes all practitioners, regardless of status or role.

Chapter 10 is a short chapter that suggests how you might now develop your writing for further purposes.

Part III
Reflecting and evaluating

Chapter 8

How is the quality of an action research text judged?

This chapter is about how the quality of your text is judged. It outlines different assessment frameworks used for judging quality in higher education study, and also identifies criteria for judging quality in areas that are specific to the writing of action research texts: these ideas may be relevant to the writing of texts for other methodologies, too.

The chapter is organised to deal with the following points:

- Which assessment frameworks are used for judging quality in higher education-level study?
- How is the quality of the action judged in action research?
- How is the quality of the research judged in action research?
- How is the quality of writing judged in higher education-level texts?
- How is your research capacity judged?

It is emphasised throughout that judging quality is a problematic area and one that needs thinking about. It is not just a case of simply achieving criteria and standards as a tick-box exercise; it is a case of showing how you are living those criteria in your practices. This means appreciating that criteria are more than words on a page: they represent real-life values. It is also emphasised that you need a sense of balance when making judgements about how the criteria and standards are to be met, and what level of knowledge and understanding is needed to make balanced judgements. I will not go into these arguments too deeply here, but they do need flagging up as issues to bear in mind.

First, consider the assessment frameworks that are widely used for making overall judgements about the quality of higher education studies.

WHICH ASSESSMENT FRAMEWORKS ARE USED FOR
JUDGING QUALITY IN HIGHER EDUCATION-LEVEL STUDY?

Undergraduate and master's study is judged in terms of university standards to ensure quality, as set out in national and international frameworks. Currently, the main framework for judging the quality of undergraduate and master's degrees in England, Wales and Northern Ireland is the *Framework for Higher Education Qualifications* (QAA, 2008). This framework sets out criteria and standards and identifies learning outcomes for students according to different levels of achievement.

Most taught programmes, including undergraduate programmes and those leading to the award of a master's degree, are organised as modules, and each module is assessed in terms of learning outcomes, that is, what you are expected to have learned and be able to do through participating in a module. Some modules are subject-specific, and some are more generalised. You are expected to show competence in the following domains (categories):

- *Knowledge and understanding*: includes aspects such as subject knowledge, use of data and evidence, capacity in research and development and understanding of ethical issues.
- *Cognitive skills and capacities*: includes aspects such as capacity in analysis, interpretation and synthesis, self-reflection and evaluation.
- *Practical skills and capacities*: includes aspects such as using your own initiative, awareness of context and uses of learning, uses of resources, communication and presentation skills, demonstration of research and social responsibility.

As an undergraduate, you will be working at Levels 5 or 6, and, as a master's-level student, at level 7. 'Level' refers to the difficulty of study, as identified by the European Qualifications Framework (EQF). Currently, levels are organised as follows:

- Level 5: foundation degrees, higher diplomas;
- Level 6: bachelor's degrees with honours, graduate certificates and graduate diplomas;
- Level 7: master's degrees, postgraduate certificates, postgraduate diplomas.

(Level 8 refers to doctoral-level study, something to aim for in the future.)

Levels of achievement expected in different knowledge domains are shown in Box 8.1. This gives an indication of how the development of research capacity is seen as a progression towards increasing levels of complexity across a domain, and capacity to theorise practices. Achievement is understood in terms of progression within levels and from one level to the next. Box 8.1 gives an example of how this works. The example is of achievement in knowledge domains.

Box 8.1 Levels of achievement in knowledge domains

- *Level 5*: Generate ideas through the analysis of concepts at an abstract level, with a command of specialised skills and the formulation of responses to well-defined and abstract problems; analyse and evaluate information; exercise significant judgement across a broad range of functions; and accept responsibility for determining and achieving personal and/or group outcomes.
- *Level 6*: Critically review, consolidate and extend a systematic and coherent body of knowledge, utilising specialised skills across an area of study; critically evaluate concepts and evidence from a range of sources; transfer and apply diagnostic and creative skills and exercise significant judgement in a range of situations; and accept accountability for determining and achieving personal and/or group outcomes.
- *Level 7*: Display mastery of a complex and specialised area of knowledge and skills, employing advanced skills to conduct research, or advanced technical or professional activity, accepting accountability.

Source: QAA (2008)

Table 8.1 on page 158 shows the EQF. Although it looks complex, it can in fact be most useful in helping you to see how different levels require a different kind of thinking. This will become clear, I hope, as the chapter progresses.

Assessment of learning is done using any or all of the following forms:

- essay assignments;
- practical reports or portfolios;
- a dissertation or other output from research/project work, which may include artefacts, performances or compositions;
- written examinations;
- oral examinations;
- problem-solving exercises;
- oral presentations;
- posters;
- placement reports.

All institutions make guidelines available to students, often in the form of student handbooks. Supervisors and mentors know where to find further information, so, if in doubt about anything, ask your supervisor.

Table 8.1 European Qualifications Framework levels

EQF levels	Knowledge and understanding	Intellectual and cognitive skill	Practical/professional skills and competence
Level 5: Foundation degrees, ordinary bachelor's degrees, higher diplomas	Comprehensive, specialised, factual and theoretical knowledge within a field of work or study and an awareness of the boundaries of that knowledge	A comprehensive range of cognitive and practical skills required to develop creative solutions to abstract problems	Exercise management and supervision in contexts of work or study activities where there is unpredictable change; review and develop performance of self and others
Level 6: Bachelor's degrees with honours, graduate certificates, graduate diplomas	Advanced knowledge of a field of work or study, involving a critical understanding of theories and principles	Advanced skills, demonstrating mastery and innovation, required to solve complex and unpredictable problems in a specialised field of work or study	Manage complex technical or professional activities or projects, taking responsibility for decision-making in unpredictable work or study contexts; take responsibility for managing professional development of individuals and groups
Level 7: Master's degrees, postgraduate certificates, postgraduate diplomas	Highly specialised knowledge, some of which is at the forefront of knowledge in a field of work or study, as the basis for original thinking and/or research. Critical awareness of knowledge issues in a field and at the interface between different fields	Specialised problem-solving skills required in research and/or innovation in order to develop new knowledge and procedures and to integrate knowledge from different fields	Manage and transform work or study contexts that are complex, unpredictable and require new strategic approaches; take responsibility for contributing to professional knowledge and practice and/or for reviewing the strategic performance of teams

However, the criteria in these guidelines can act only as indicators for making judgements about quality. Also, specific things need to be addressed when judging quality in action research and practice-based research in general. Here are some of the things your reader wishes to see.

They wish to see a demonstration of your understanding that, although the words 'action research' always go together to form a conceptual unit, you can focus on the action and the research separately in order to make judgements about them when assessing the overall quality of the range of practices narrated in a text. They also want to see your understanding that making judgements of any kind is a matter of ethics. By making a judgement, you are effectively saying, 'This is the right thing to do'. They especially want to see your understanding that, although 'good' can mean 'high quality', quality is always linked with ethics, and that different people, including yourself, usually have different views about what counts as 'good' (ethical) behaviour. One person's idea of 'the good' may be another person's idea of the 'not so good'. So, they do not want to see comments in your text to the effect, 'I think my practice was good', or, 'The situation was resolved', which communicate a glib and uncritical perspective. They also do not wish to read, 'I made this happen'. They would prefer to see you holding your knowledge lightly and remaining open to new possibilities and an acknowledgement that you have contributed to improvement in some way, but that you did not do it alone. You enlisted the support of others on the basis that all are able and should be invited to contribute, and that shared understandings may be taken as the basis for shared and other-oriented practices.

So, let's now focus specifically on the action element of your action research, bearing in mind, however, that the action and the research always go together.

HOW IS THE QUALITY OF THE ACTION JUDGED IN ACTION RESEARCH?

Whatever stories about your actions you choose to tell in your text, you need to show your awareness that you are always in the company of other people, and it is the relationships with those people that give your life meaning. Although the 'I' is the focus of action research, the story is not about 'me', in a self-centred way. It is about myself in relation with others who are their own selves: we are all in this together. Also, when people come together they become more than individual selves: they become a different kind of entity, each influencing and being influenced by the others, and this gives them a special shared form of understanding and power. Arendt (1958) said that, when power goes into the hands of people who use it against others, it is no longer power but becomes violence. Power is only power when it is in the hands of people who wish to do something about their situations and improve matters for all, as appropriate. Because doing action research is always collaborative, it is, therefore, always about generating power for people. An important action is the process of trying to understand other people and acting in appropriate ways.

This is where it is essential for you to explain how you make judgements about the quality of your actions. We noted above that the criteria in official documents act as indicators or guidelines as to what kinds of behaviour and understanding readers wish to see. The criteria reflect what is assumed to be 'good': they reflect your values. Your reader hopes to see your understanding that you have turned abstract concepts such as 'collaboration' into meaningful actions, so that you can say that you have realised your values

Example 35

Here is an extract from the report of the Time to Listen project, conducted with two other researchers in Northern Ireland, as part of then newly introduced Education for Mutual Understanding curriculum.

> Cooperative practices were evident throughout the evaluation process. It involved, as did the wider Time to Listen project, the systematic gathering of data, monitoring of practice, reflection on the data and the generation of evidence. For the evaluation process we used many of the same data gathering techniques as in the project: reflective diaries, observations, field notes, conversations. Jean, who had been contracted to lead the evaluation process, conducted tape recorded conversations together with Mary Rose, the Project Officer, with teachers and supporters. Jean transcribed the tapes, which were given back to participants for their editing and approval. However, she as much as anyone else systematically reflected on her practice and invited critical feedback on how she might do things differently.
>
> This was evident in the process of writing up. Kushner (2000) speaks about the evaluator who is positioned as a friend during the data gathering process but who becomes a scientist for the writing up of the report. This transformation can involve a betrayal of the participants. I, Jean, refused to see myself in this light. I was a friend during the project, and I intended to remain a friend during the writing up of the report. Therefore, while I accepted the responsibility of drafting the report, the report itself was distributed to all participants before publication for their approval, editing and rewriting. All participants were invited to speak. I am not naive about the kinds of power relationships which exist between academics and teachers, and between professional evaluators and participants; and how people say what they believe those with supposedly 'higher' status wish them to say; but I really believe that our group did reach a considerable degree of parity of esteem and all felt able to say what they wished, without fear of recrimination.
>
> Time to Listen project, 2015

in practice. You can say you are engaging in collaborative practices and you can show the realities of what you are doing. This means gathering data and generating evidence to show what is happening. Further, when you claim that these are your values, it does not mean that you impose your values on others. It means that you check with others if you are right in thinking as you do and are prepared to negotiate your values and accept the responsibility of holding them. This in itself brings huge dilemmas, because you do have to take a stand in life and declare that some actions are unacceptable, such as wanton cruelty, no matter what the circumstances. However, people can be cruel, and this is a fact of life (see Example 35 on page 160).

So what are examiners looking for?

It is this kind of critical perspective that examiners are looking for and that will get you high marks. If you say, 'We developed collaborative practices', and leave it at that, it is unlikely that your examiner will take you seriously. You need to show your understanding of (a) the actions you took and (b) your reasons and purposes in taking them. And, because this is a scholarly text, you also need to show engagement with the literatures around these matters. Look, for example, at the work of Richard Winter (1989), who says that action enquiries should demonstrate at least these qualities:

* reflexive critique: the capacity to reflect critically on one's own work and see its limitations as well as its strengths;
* dialectical critique: the capacity to appreciate the social, cultural and historical contexts in which the work is done; the need for cultural sensitivity and awareness of the other's needs;
* collaborative resource: participants in the research act as resources for one another;
* risk: action research is inherently risky, because you have to accept that you never know the consequences of actions; nevertheless you take action with the intent of contributing to other people's flourishing;
* plural structure: action research cannot be an isolationist practice, as it always involves other people, who have minds of their own;
* theory, practice, transformation: theory and practice are intertwined; practice is the basis of new theory, and new theory feeds back into practice.

I have examined many texts where a candidate has said that they were collaborative, but sometimes all I see is the word 'collaborative'. With luck, I also see descriptions of episodes of practice where people worked together. Ideally, however, I am looking for a critical interrogation of what 'collaborative' might look like in action.

For me, this is how the action element of action research should be judged. An author should explain what actions they took, why they took them, and what they hoped to achieve. They also need to say how they negotiated these actions with others. There are no abstract actions in life: actions are always what we do in relation, either to ourselves as an internal dialogue, or to others in social dialogues. This needs to be said in the text with, if possible, a note about why it is important to say it.

This could be seen as the distinction that separates good from adequate in writing. It is the capacity to show the transformation of abstract concepts into meaningful actions – that is, the realisation of values into practices – and, given that making judgements is also an action, it shows how you have negotiated your values position with others without necessarily compromising those values. You can say you are collaborative, but this does not mean that you are, or that you act in a way that other people would wish you to. Further, you need to gather data and generate evidence, which also needs to be authenticated, to show that you are being collaborative in the sense that you genuinely sought out others' opinions about your actions. It is this kind of critique that examiners are looking for and that will get you high marks.

However, remember: according to Loy (2010; see Chapter 4), this is a story too.

Example 36

In 2009, colleagues from York St John University and I convened a critical debate session at the annual meeting of the British Educational Research Association. Jenny Carpenter, a member of the team, communicates her initial doubts about whether or not she was exercising her educational influence in students' learning. She writes:

> As part of the planning for the primary PGCE programme, I was keen to establish student reflection as a core element. This could be achieved through encouraging an enquiry-based approach to learning conversations with students and school-based mentors during teaching placements. I was, however, surprised at the lack of interest by the students, and their reluctance to engage critically with their own learning, especially from my understanding that developing the capacity for reflexive critique and dialectical critique are taken as key criteria for judging the quality of action-oriented enquiries (Winter, 1989). I found myself asking key questions: Why did students not see the value of being involved in their own learning? Why did they not see themselves as on a learning journey, as I did? I became increasingly aware of the need to reflect critically on my own understanding of my practice with regard to the relationship between my actions, values and role as course leader, and on the basis that I was striving to realise my values in my practice (Whitehead, 1989).
>
> Carpenter, 2015

Now, let's see how these ideas manifest also in the research element of action research.

HOW IS THE QUALITY OF THE RESEARCH JUDGED IN ACTION RESEARCH?

Think about what constitutes the research element of action research and how its quality may be demonstrated and assessed.

In Chapter 1, we looked at the main aspects of doing all kinds of research: this means being able (among other things) to:

- state the reasons and purposes of the research, which include creating new knowledge and making claims to knowledge, testing the validity of knowledge claims and generating new theory;
- state the means of achieving the purposes, which includes articulating the methodologies used in the research and the reasons for selecting these methodologies;
- explain the significance of what has been achieved, which includes critical reflection and reframing of thinking and action in light of the evaluation.

Demonstrating quality of research, therefore, means showing that you have done all these things and can explain why you have done them and what you hope to achieve. You can do this by making clear throughout your report or dissertation how you engage with relevant issues to demonstrate:

- methodological rigour;
- ethical conduct through your own positioning in the research;
- the need for critique.

Consider each of these points in more depth.

Demonstrating methodological rigour

Stenhouse (1983) spoke about research as 'a systematic enquiry made public'. In 2002 and 2013, I added, 'with social intent', because, in my view, research should always be done for a social purpose; it is never undertaken outside a social context.

The idea of systematic enquiry is important. 'Systematic' does not imply a one-dimensional procedure: it implies more the idea that you can use imaginative designs and processes, provided you can show how the whole maintains coherence in relation to its parts. It is your job to demonstrate the integrity of the research and the internal discipline of the processes involved (its rigour). We said earlier that you write your knowledge claim (what you have found out through doing the research) on the first page, and possibly even in the first paragraph of the text, and then spend the rest of the text demonstrating how you have tested the validity (truthfulness) of the knowledge claim. The story of action becomes the golden thread that runs through the text. At the end, you still have no guarantee that your reader will believe your claim, but you can be satisfied that you have made a strong enough case to justify what Dewey (1963) called 'warranted belief'.

Imagine that, as you write your text, in the same way as when you walk or run the length of a course, you see at intervals a series of markers, or landmarks, that tell you where you are and how far you have to go. Each marker has advice written on it, explaining what you need to do to achieve specific aspects at that point. As you move forward, you read the advice on each of the markers, as follows:

- Marker 1: Identify a research issue here.
- Marker 2: Now identify research aims.
- Marker 3: Formulate a research question here.
- Marker 4: Check that you have set out a research design.
- Marker 5: Now write a section about monitoring practice and gathering data to show the situation as it is at the moment: do that here.
- Marker 6: Stop here for 2 minutes. Think about what to do and consider what actions you should take.
- Marker 7: Remember to identify criteria and standards to analyse and make sense of the data as you gather it, and so on.

A useful strategy is to draw a cartoon strip to show systematic progress along your route.

Noting and using markers such as these can give you an outline plan for your report or dissertation. When you write up your story, your reader can see that you did all these things in a systematic way. They read a story of how you:

- identified a research issue;
- articulated your research aims;
- formulated a research question;
- set out a research design;
- monitored practice and gathered data to show the situation as it was;
- thought about what to do and took appropriate action;
- identified criteria and standards to analyse and make sense of the data;
- continued to monitor practice, gather data and generate evidence in relation to your identified criteria and standards of judgement;
- made a provisional claim to knowledge;
- linked the claim with existing knowledge (as in the literatures);
- tested the validity of the claim through submitting it to critique;
- explained the potential significance of the research and claim;
- generated theory from the research;
- modified practice in light of the evaluation;

- wrote a report and disseminated findings;
- commented on whether the whole process had contributed to improving the quality of life for yourself and others.

Through developing understandings of the systematic nature of research, you are also able to show how action and research inform and transform into each other. Action is seen as a form of research; research is seen as an action-oriented process. They are always together and interweave as mutually reciprocal practices.

Now, consider how and why all these elements need to be seen as ethical, mainly through how you position yourself in relation with others.

Demonstrating ethical conduct through your own positioning in the research

As well as identifying markers along the methodological pathway, you also need to consider how you do this. Do you walk alone, or with another person? How do you see that person – as someone who carries your bag, or as a companion, a fellow traveller? If you see them as a bag carrier, you probably see them as a means to your ends, whereas, if you see them as a companion, you see them as ends in themselves, people who belong to themselves. This has a direct bearing on how you position yourself and others in the research.

Eikeland (2006) points out the importance of critiquing the idea of 'communities of practice'. He suggests that the concept of 'communities of enquiry' may be more appropriate for action research (or possibly any kind of research). A community of practice consists of people who share the same practice, but this does not necessarily mean that their engagement in the practice is dialogical or excludes hierarchical relationships. Autocratic people can share the same community of practice as self-effacing people; a hierarchically ordered prison can represent the context for a community of practice. A community of enquiry is something else; if everyone is enquiring and finding ways of doing things better, they are all learning, and learning is a great leveller. The community of people who share the same intent of learning is a context where everyone acknowledges that they do not know and wish to find ways of coming to know. People who position themselves like this in relation to others are more likely to demonstrate ethical behaviour than others who adopt superior attitudes. Eikeland takes the view that the relationships in conventional social science, and in many kinds of action research, demonstrate what he calls a form of 'condescending ethics', where those who position themselves as superior to others give a passing nod to the need for ethical behaviours and then walk on. Issues like these are considered by Jenny Carpenter in Example 37 on page 166.

Example 37

Jenny Carpenter continues (from the previous box):

> However, I again encountered moral dilemmas, which seemed at the time
> to conflict with my educational values. My management and pedagogical
> aims were to develop my capacity for pedagogical and academic leadership,
> and to communicate that the programme would operate smoothly partly
> by reassuring the students that they were in capable hands. These became
> my guiding leadership and management values. However, I came to
> wonder whether I was imposing my values system on my students. Would
> they feel coerced into agreeing with me against their better judgements,
> and possibly in areas where their values were contrary to my own? Through
> engaging with these problematics, and through drawing on the literatures,
> I have come to understand that values need to be negotiated, and that there
> are few overarching universal values (Berlin, 1969). Further, I have come
> to the realisation that I need to problematise the question of values, and
> perhaps understand values as practices rather than as abstract principles
> (Raz, 2003).

Now, return to the idea of the need to demonstrate critique in all the spaces
of doing research.

Demonstrating the need for critique

There are no straightforward answers to the questions, 'What is good? How
do we behave?' I was once on a panel of four speakers at a conference, where
a question was asked, 'Do you need to get a specific outcome in action
research?' Two members of the panel said yes; the other two, including me,
said no. If the aim is to produce a specific outcome or result, then action
research becomes a kind of instrumental social science research that works
on an 'if . . . then' basis. To me, action research is about learning and being
prepared to accept that some things cannot be resolved and you have to do
the best with what you have. I prefer the perspective of philosophers such
as Dewey (1963) that the only 'outcome' of learning is more learning. In my
view, some dilemmas in life defy simple resolution. Ownership of the Dome
of the Rock in Jerusalem is claimed by both Jews and Arabs; the issue is not
that one is seen as right and the other wrong, so much as a situation of
competing rights. Human dilemmas like this are everywhere and cannot be
resolved through simple technical decisions.

By the same token, action research is not about problem-solving, but more
about problem posing: it is more important to ask questions than to provide
answers. A major problem with the literatures of action research these days

is that many appear to be about providing answers – possibly because a lot of action research has been hijacked by higher education (see Chapter 1), whose aim, in these days of neo-liberalism and marketisation, is to promote the illusion of concrete answers rather than encourage discernment and problematisation.

However, this is my view and represents my story, which I am assuming is better than someone else's. I am in danger of becoming fundamentalist – 'My way of life, my idea, my god, is better than yours' – and fundamentalist thinking is dangerous: it is not only wrong, but also carries the power of conviction that insists that it is right. But this is also a story, and I have become quite fundamentalist in stating it and have denied my own values and rhetoric. What to do? Do we come down on one side or another, or adopt an attitude that says anything goes?

Many authors, and I agree, believe that it is important to adopt a critical perspective. Said, for example, asks, 'How does one speak the truth? What truth? For whom and where?' (Said, 1994: 65). He says:

> I take criticism so seriously that, even in the very midst of a battle in which one is unmistakably on one side against another, there should be criticism, because there must be critical consciousness if there are to be issues, problems, values, even lives to be fought for.
>
> (Said, 1991: 28)

But this is a story too. And, if a story is always embedded within another story, you can go in circles of ever-diminishing regress without any guidance other than to do what seems right at the time. You have to take a stand somewhere, otherwise the spiral of stories will paralyse you into inactivity. Also, in books such as this, it is not fair to raise deep dilemmas without stating one's own position, so I will now state mine.

I have learned the importance of challenging my own thinking. Any answer seems to generate new questions, and I hold multiple conflicting values. I believe in freedom, yet recognise that one person's freedom may mean the denial of another's. My freedom to use your chair denies your freedom to use it. Which values do we use to work out matters such as this?

So, while I see the need for critique, I also see the need to make a stand about principles. For me, wanton cruelty can never be condoned, nor can the practice of suttee, where widows are required to throw themselves on the funeral pyre of their dead husband. I challenge hypocrisy in all its forms, including in myself, especially when it is dressed up in the garb of false consciousness, where people are led to believe they brought their misfortunes on themselves and it was their idea to do so in the first place. This, for me, is often the manifestation of position power; when intellectuals do it, it is all the more serious. Lilla (2001) tells of how Heidegger lent his intellectual powers to the Nazis, which Lilla sees as an abuse of intellect and a waste of giftedness.

So, to return to the need for criticality in action research, as well as demonstrating social aspects such as collaboration, a text needs to demonstrate critical intellectual and emotional aspects, such as interrogation and decentring. This is what your examiners are hoping to see. It means being critical in that you engage with, and possibly challenge, what authors say in the literatures, and that you engage with and challenge your own thinking. It means that you actually do step through the mirror and question what is normatively assumed to be 'right' and what gives the speaker the right to say so.

HOW IS THE QUALITY OF WRITING JUDGED IN HIGHER EDUCATION-LEVEL TEXTS?

As noted in Chapters 3 and 4, a main criterion for judging the quality of a text as a text is in terms of whether it is written for a reader. This may be judged by the clarity of writing, which leads to effectiveness of communication. These also become two main criteria.

Your examiner will expect to see the following characteristics in your writing:

Style of language

- The language used is appropriate to the audience for which it is intended. Do not try to be too clever when writing: state things in a clear and simple fashion.
- The language is grammatical. This includes paying attention to punctuation, as well as to spellings and correct syntax. If you don't understand a word, leave it out. Use a dictionary and a thesaurus. You can find plenty of these online too.
- Edit your work ruthlessly. Read it often. If it does not read well to you, it will not read well to your reader. Change anything that does not move along effortlessly.
- Check for accuracy of statements. Get your facts right.
- Proofread often. Proofread many times. If you are not good at proofreading, engage the services of a professional proofreader or copy-editor (a copy-editor checks things such as layout and grammar; a proofreader checks that everything is spelled correctly, pages are correctly numbered and no words are missing).
- Concepts are explained coherently and succinctly. If you are developing an argument, make sure you set it out clearly so that your reader can follow it. Use link words and phrases to make it hang together.
- Use the active voice throughout. Avoid saying 'not only ... but also ...'. Say instead 'both ... and ...'.
- Change your style from time to time, to keep your reader alert. Sometimes write in short points (as I am doing here) and at others write continuous prose. You can also use poetry or pictures, as appropriate to your text. Variety makes the text interesting and holds everyone's attention.
- Let your enthusiasm for your topic come through, but don't get carried away. Stay disciplined. A kind anonymous reviewer of my very first book said of my tendency to be overcritical of authors with whom I disagreed,

'If this is the kind of language she uses to critique research accounts, what kind of language does she reserve for the likes of Pol Pot?' Another reviewer, as recently as 2013, suggested as an amendment to an article that, 'the conclusion should be stated more modestly'. I think I had said that my research demonstrated that the point I was making was achievable and that I had achieved it. We learn through experience. The most important point perhaps is that we remain open to learning. And I did make the conclusion more modest.

Appearance of the text

- The appearance of the text should be clean and uncluttered. Make sure you leave sufficient room for margins and between sections.
- Set out your section headings in a systematic fashion. Use different fonts and weights to indicate whether you are using an 'A', 'B' or 'C' heading. Try not to use more than three types of heading, otherwise your text will be too cluttered, and your reader may get confused. Headings are important signposts that keep your reader (and you) on track.
- It can help to produce notes for the structure of your chapter before you write it. You can also write a summary in the form of a set of bullet points at the beginning of a chapter to say what it will contain ('This chapter contains the following points: . . .'). Check back to make sure you have not missed out a section in the text that you indicated in the introductory points.
- Also include a summary at the ends of chapters to remind your reader of what you have said. It should be possible for a reader to read the introductory notes and summary of a chapter and get a good sense of what it contains. The rest of the text is devoted to developing arguments and explaining what you did in your research and how and why you did it.
- The first thing your reader notes when they pick up your work is its appearance. It is in your interests to ensure that it looks attractive and inviting, something that you would not mind reading yourself. If you don't like any aspect of your work, neither will your reader.

Academic criteria

- Reference works accurately. Check that all works cited in the text appear in the list of references. Print out a separate list of references, or put it on your computer screen, and tick off each reference as it appears in the text. If in doubt about a date or publisher, ask your supervisor or librarian. Get it right. Readers will forgive a few minor slippages, but not many. Getting references right is a sign of your professionalism: don't compromise it.
- Don't make derogatory remarks about works you have read. If you can't say something positive, even though it may be critical, don't say anything.

- Cite primary sources whenever possible, especially when developing an argument that is central to your study. Use secondary sources for indicating new thinking or where you wish to focus in future.
- Make sure the order in which you write citations is correct. The order should be: Author's family name [Brown], initial of first name [J.], date [(2014)], title of publication [*The Life of Birds in Scotland*], town of publication [Aberdeen], name of publishers [Pink Press]. Study how textbooks and journals set out their lists of references and copy them. If in doubt, ask your librarian or supervisor.
- Make sure your title page is set out as per the instructions in your student handbook. Make sure you include a date and word count. Check whether there is a standard format for title pages and stick with it.
- Keep any acknowledgements fuss-free.
- Get your work bound professionally. Make it look good. You owe it to yourself and those who have supported you.

HOW IS YOUR RESEARCH CAPACITY JUDGED?

So far, we have considered the text, but in fact your text is an extension of you. You communicate your personal and professional values through your writing, in the same way as through the way that you dress or speak. Your text is your window to the world: you show how you see the world through your writing, and you also invite the world to see you. When people make judgements about your writing, they are actually making judgements about you as a person.

Look at the last column of the EQF levels in Table 8.1, 'Practical/ professional skills and competence'. The advice given there, about managing complex situations, refers directly to your professional context, and this includes the professional context of researching your writing and the production of your text. Through reading your text, your reader will come to judgements about you. They will especially ask:

- Does this person demonstrate research capacity? Do they show that they have undertaken basic research training and know, for example, how to reference works and how to set quotations in a text? Do they know that quotations need a page reference as well as a name and date, and need to be indented after 40 words? In terms of the content of the text, do they show that they know, for example, how to code and analyse data, how to do a literature review and the need for substantiated conclusions? Do they show that they are aware of the standards required at their level?
- Does this person show that they have tenacity and perseverance in producing a text of consistently good literary and academic quality? Chitra Divakaruni (2003), the award-winning novelist, tells how she had to read more than 300 books when judging for the National Book Awards. She says that what distinguished a good book from a mediocre book was consistency of quality throughout.

- Do they show their professionalism in ensuring that the text itself is of high literary merit? Have they taken care in proofreading? Do they show that they are serious about doing research and that they have a passion for enquiry?

If the answer to all the questions is 'Yes', you can be confident that you are on the way to achieving your award.

Summary

This chapter has considered how the quality of your work may be judged according to different sets of criteria and expectations. It has first outlined what the official guidelines recommend in terms of structures and marking schemes, before moving on to consider how the quality of your text is judged in relation to the action and the research of action research, and the quality of writing. Ultimately, all these aspects lead to how you, the action researcher, are judged in relation to your capacity to carry out an action enquiry and to produce a text that will help you achieve your desired goals.

Chapter 9, the next chapter, offers ideas about the overall significance of your work and writing, with some possible implications.

Chapter 9

The significance of your writing

If you go into the offices of the *Chicago Tribune* newspaper and stand in the great entrance hall, you will see writing on the walls, words everywhere. On the south wall, you can read:

> *A free press stands as one of the great interpreters between the government and the people. To allow it to be fettered is to fetter ourselves.*
> – An opinion handed down on Feb. 11, 1936, by Associate Judge George Sutherland and concurred in unanimously by the U.S. Supreme Court in the case of Grossjean vs. The American Press.

Also on the south wall:

> *The liberty of opinion depends on the freedom of the press and that can not be limited without being lost.*
> – Thomas Jefferson, third president of the United States and chief framer of the Declaration of Independence.

On the north wall, you read:

> *Where there is a free press the governors must live in constant awe of the opinions of the governed.*
> – Thomas Babington Macaulay, 19th century British essayist, historian, poet and statesman.

To the east and west, the same, words that spell out the liberty and entitlement of ordinary people to write, and caution to anyone who positions themselves as a ruler.

This chapter is about the significance of your writing. Sometimes, people do not see why they should write, or what its use value would be. Think again. Your writing is possibly the most powerful asset you can have, more powerful than status or position or even qualifications, though qualifications can help. Your writing is more than you. It speaks for generations.

When you tell people that you are researching your practice as a writer, they sometimes say, 'Really? Oh, yes, but what's the point? You are a plumber'. These are important words to hear, because they mean you have to think about who you are and what is special about the fact that you are learning how to write well. You are learning how to communicate more effectively, and this is significant for many dimensions. These include the personal (for yourself and your practice), the professional (for your colleagues and for your organisational practices) and the political (for your profession and for the wider world). I am using the term 'dimension', as derived from Noffke (2009: 8), to refer to 'the multiple layers of assumptions, purposes and practices' involved. As in the rest of the book, I adopt these layers to write ideas, and I organise the chapter to reflect them, as follows:

- The personal significance of your writing;
- The professional and organisational significance of your writing;
- The political significance of your writing.

Each of these areas is significant for its own context, and beyond, into the next. The personal transforms into the professional and organisational, which in turn transforms into the political. When you write for yourself, you are potentially writing for the world.

Here are some ideas about the significance of your writing for all three dimensions.

THE PERSONAL SIGNIFICANCE OF YOUR WRITING

First, consider the lovely idea of faith in the work of words. This idea comes from Eric Doxtader (2009), who writes about some of the processes in South Africa, from 1983 to 1995, that led to the Truth and Reconciliation Commission. He writes: 'In the name of a beginning, reconciliation begins with a belief that there are words which hold the potential for all things to become new' (Doxtader, 2009: ix). The 'new' for him is how to bring together warring factions to create a new democratic civil order that respects all humans' rights. His question is, 'How do words of reconciliation transform human relationships?' (page x). The 'new' for me is how practitioners can produce their theories of practice and disseminate them through their writings to create a new knowledge base that will influence the thinking of others, across professions and other social formations, and through time. These writings show how action research has moved away from mainly researcher-centric forms and developed increasingly towards collaborative, other-oriented practices. This shift is gathering momentum globally, especially through new forms of social networking, greatly assisted by technology.

Consider also that all personal and social change begins in the individual and collective mind. In a famous comment in relation to the peace process in Northern Ireland, when there was deadlock about the need for prior decommissioning by the IRA in order to reach agreement, John Hume, then leader of the SDLP, observed that decommissioning begins in the mind rather than in the laying down of arms. I agree. I think the same understanding extends to the significance of your action research, and of your writing. Change begins in your mind, and in the minds of those you work with and influence, and through your willingness equally to be influenced by them. This is a dialogical practice. By finding ways to communicate the idea of change to others through the practice of writing, you deliberately signal to them that you are both a competent practitioner and a capable theorist. This happens in the following ways.

Demonstrating that you are a competent practitioner

Action and research always take place in the practice area. In relation to writing, they take place in the collaborative practices of people and the production of texts. Producing a text tends to be done by an individual, frequently working alone, but always drawing on and acknowledging collaborative work undertaken with others in social and workplace settings. This collaboration happens in two dimensions: horizontally through space, where you work with people in your current contexts, and vertically through time, where you work with other people from earlier experiences. At this current point of horizontal collaboration, you have asked, 'How do I improve my practice in my workplace?', and collectively you have asked, 'How do we improve our practices in our workplaces?' Now, by asking, 'How do I improve my practice as a writer?', you show how you have learned to communicate the significance of those workplace practices through writing. You have developed knowledge of writing practice in terms of the following:

- Know-that (factual knowledge): you demonstrate know-that because you have studied substantive, discipline-based issues. You can show what it means to have developed your learning about dentistry or carpentry.
- Know-how (procedural knowledge): you show how you have developed skills and competencies appropriate to your field and discipline.
- Know-why: explanatory knowledge, which incorporates know-that and know-how: you can say what you know, how you have come to know it across knowledge domains, and why it is important to know these things. You show and explain the integration of your different knowledges through the unity of your text.

You can also show and explain that you have developed communicative competence. You know the differences between telling a story and communicating with a reader. You can comment on what these different perspectives mean in the real world, and how they can be achieved. You can comment on the quality of your learning and show how your learning has contributed to the improvement of your own and others' practices. You may well have involved others in your practice, and you can show how they have, in turn, learned how to improve the quality of their practice, too, possibly through your influence, and can make considered judgements about how they understand 'the good'. You can explain how and why this kind of transformational practice, where you pass on your knowledge to others responsibly, has potential for personal and social good, especially in terms of contributing to your own and others' flourishing, as well as to the sustainability of your organisation and profession.

Demonstrating that you are a capable theorist

Through studying your practice, and explaining what you are doing and why you are doing it, you can show how you have generated your personal theory of practice. You can ground your claims to having done this by referring to a rigorously authenticated evidence base where you can show that you have fulfilled specific academic demands. You have gathered data and analysed them in relation to the values you have identified as central to informing your practices. Those values have now come to act as the criteria you use to decide what counts as quality in the practices you are speaking about.

You have organised the data into a systematic evidence base that explicitly shows the processes involved and demonstrates how you have developed your practices to a high practical level. You are able to explain how this practice-based form of theory is appropriate for judging quality in work-based learning. Further, because you are now placing your text into the academic field, you show how practice-based forms of theory can come to stand as high-quality academic theory. You have deconstructed (and demolished) the practitioner–academic theoretical divide (see Example 39 on page 177).

You may experience the same dilemmas over how you understand your identity. However, through producing a text that contains your personal theory of practice, you can show that you have added value to the concept of theorising identity and other practices in general. You have exercised your right to research, which Appadurai (2006) says is the responsibility of professionals, and you now show that you are qualified to engage in public discourses about what counts as valid practice-based knowledge and about who is entitled to be seen as a researcher and a theorist. Thereby, you also show your responsibility to research.

Further, you can show how you have engaged with your own thinking and can challenge orthodox views about what counts as valid academic knowledge. You think for yourself as a person claiming originality of thinking (Polanyi, 1958) and willing to make your contribution with political intent. This has considerable implications for what counts as professionalism and how professionals may understand themselves and their disciplinary fields (see Example 38 page 176).

Example 38

Alex Sinclair, a university-based teacher educator of science, is now pursuing his own doctoral studies. He writes about the significance of his learning through beginning to write up his action research:

> For me, the most interesting, but potentially most difficult element in conducting action research has been my evolving understanding of the ontological and epistemological underpinnings of this form of research. This evolution can be demonstrated by briefly outlining a shift in my way of thinking in three interdependent ways. The first has been due to having spent much of my life being schooled in the propositional world of science and science teaching where knowledge is often deemed fixed and static. It has been a revelation to explore that this standpoint can be challenged and that knowledge claims can only be made tentatively and with a degree of uncertainty. In parallel with this is my ongoing appreciation of my role within the knowledge-creation process. I appreciate that I am not involved in a linear, one way flow of facts but now view myself symbiotically linked to others in relational epistemologies. And finally, it is only through doing action research that I have come to recognise the importance of practitioners creating their own theories and that theory-making is not just left to academics in 'ivory towers'. These new ways of working have not come easily and have taken time to develop. I fully expect that were I to undertake writing this paragraph at another point that my response would be different to mirror my, inevitable, future new way of thinking.
>
> (Sinclair, 2013, doctoral study writings)

Such texts show their authors' faith in the work of words, both in their work-based practice settings and in the desk-based practice settings where they have produced their texts. They are defined by their words, and their words define them.

THE PROFESSIONAL AND ORGANISATIONAL SIGNIFICANCE OF YOUR WRITING

Through making your personal research public, you can show how engaging in research can contribute to raising the profile of your profession, especially through your commitment to collaborative working practices. You are showing how knowledge is not the preserve only of established academic elites, but is also generated by, and therefore belongs to, practitioners who have studied their practices and are willing to make these studies public through the production of texts.

Example 39

Jane Rand sought to challenge the theory-practice divide through her studies. Here, she reflects on her experience both as a student on an EdD course and on entering the Post Compulsory Education Training (PCET) sector as a new tutor, where she initially struggled with her professional identity. She says:

> As an 'insider' interpretive researcher (Sikes and Potts, 2008), exploring my positionality within my EdD thesis was essential. I recognised in myself a personal dissatisfaction with the concept of an academic/vocational divide in post-compulsory education. I have had the privilege of working with many who have embarked on 'post-school', other than university-based, learning, ranging in ages, experience, confidence, qualifications, ambition and self-belief. Almost all of these people would have described themselves as 'not academic'. As a learner myself, I first engaged with higher education as a mature student, having chosen a post-school route which included both full-time further education and, later, a combination of work and part-time study in further education. Later still, I left the world of work to study in higher education full-time. I returned to work, in a second career, as a teacher in the post-compulsory education and training sector. In this time, my own learning 'diet' included both subject-specific and pedagogical scholarship. In contrast to those learners I have worked with in post-school settings, I did not consider myself in terms of being 'academic', 'not academic', or 'vocational. . . .
>
> What I particularly learned about myself was that (perhaps in contrast to some of my PCET colleagues) my scholarly activity was closely linked to a desire to satisfy an internal(ised) concern about the validity of me occupying a professional role. Writing a researcher identity memo led me to explore a feeling of insecurity I had early in my second career related to validating my position as a Further Education lecturer through 'academic' credentials, in the absence of (academic) experience. Memoing enabled me to explore a personal transition from an early focus on quantifiable academic achievement (suggesting my own experiential residue was highly influenced by quantification/credentialism) to a distinct qualitative under-pinning to my scholarship and practice. As a result, I became aware of my highly reflective and reflexive approach to developing myself as a researcher. Memoing revealed the deep-seated nature of the value I place on retaining, and promoting scholarship within post-compulsory education, and within post-compulsory Initial Teacher Education. Without scholar-ship, PCET and PCET ITE risks becoming 'dumbed down'. I saw my com-plementary role as a teacher–educator and active scholar as pivotal in championing the scholarship and professionalism associated with teaching in the sector, regardless of whether a subject-specialism might typically be considered as 'academic' or 'vocational'.
>
> (Rand, 2016)

These kinds of publication could have far-reaching implications for all professions, many of which are directed (and owned) by a small group of research-active, publications-active elites. They are especially important when thinking about the idea of a knowledge base. A knowledge base comprises the texts that have been produced by the profession for the profession. Therefore, because those elites are virtually the only people who actively publish their work, messages are communicated through the media that they own the knowledge base of the profession. Through claiming ownership of the knowledge base, they control the knowledge; and through controlling the knowledge, they by default own the profession. It is a nice example of Dyrberg's (1997) view of the closed circular structure of power. However, you can challenge this situation through demonstrating your capacity to write too. You can write and publish your accounts of practice. Further, by involving others and encouraging them to produce their research accounts too, you collectively demonstrate the power of collaborative working for social, including organisational, improvement. Through the encouragement of all by all to make their research public, there is a strong chance that the existing knowledge base may be opened up and transformed into one that is also created and managed by the local professional workforce.

This is a most important point, with extensive implications. Currently, and as noted above, the knowledge bases of the majority of professions comprise accounts written by the same elites that control the profession. To extend Dyrberg's (1997) vision of the circular structure of power, legitimisation processes are also managed such that they legitimise themselves, an inward-looking form of regress. However, objectively speaking, this situation is unhealthy for all social formations, including professions. It has been demonstrated in a range of fields, including business and economics, that a system tends to collapse without internal or external critique. Possibly the only way to rescue such a system from self-annihilation is to introduce a strategy of critique so that new perspectives are deliberately developed to challenge existing ways. This means injecting fresh ideas into established scenarios, monitoring how they work, imagining new solutions to practical dilemmas, taking action and evaluating outcomes – in other words, doing action research in organisational settings.

This kind of deliberate strategic action can contribute to the new kind of professionalism you are aiming for where, rather than critique being seen as superfluous or potentially damaging to the system, it is established as integral to the health and ongoing well-being of the system and to be encouraged (see Example 40 on page 179).

Your research and the text through which you give an account of your work contribute to this value-added critique of the current system of what counts as professional knowledge and, therefore, what counts as professionalism. You are demonstrating your professional responsibility by making your contribution to this new knowledge base. You are making your research public for others to adopt or adapt, as they wish. You are also showing, by this making public, that you have worked on improving your capacity as a

Example 40

Here is an example of what such critique might look like. It is also another demonstration of faith in the work of words.

In an account stemming from the fourth annual Value and Virtue in Practice-Based Research conference at York St John University (the main themes of which were openness and criticality), Jon Nixon and colleagues focus on what it means to work collaboratively with and through words. Although it is widely recognised that collaborative working is virtually a requirement in action research approaches (see page 23), it is not so widely understood what collaborative writing means or how it can be managed. Jon and colleagues show what collaborative writing can look like and how it might be achieved.

The text begins:

> This chapter developed from a number of conversations that took place at the 4th International Conference on Value and Virtue in Practice-Based Research the twin themes of which were 'openness' and 'criticality'. These chance and often fleeting conversations focused on ideas explored in the keynote address that Jon delivered at the conference, but spanned out into a wider discussion of the relevance of those ideas within different arenas of professional practice.
>
> After the conference we agreed via email that [the contributors] Alison, Andy, Jane, Jonathan and Sue would respond – from their different perspectives and value orientations – to the ideas explored in Jon's keynote. How might these ideas translate into professional practice? How might embedded practice speak back to the generality of these ideas? How do the ideas relate to our core values as educators involved in practice-based research?
>
> These were our starting points. They have resulted in the following edited version of Jon's original address interlaced with questions and interjections from the co-authors of this chapter. We are not claiming that what follows is dialogical, but it does attempt to open up a conversation on the nature of understanding and what it means to be someone who seeks to understand.
>
> Jon began his address with a quotation from the philosopher Hans-Georg Gadamer: *'And what is hermeneutical imagination? It is a sense of the questionableness of something and what this requires of us'* (Gadamer, 2004, 41–42).
>
> (Nixon *et al.*, 2016)

The text then takes the form of a conversation, where Jon makes a point about the questions he poses above, to which others respond out of their own interpretations of the point. Jon doesn't position himself as 'the knower', more as a learner who is aspiring to know, and to come to know better through the company of others. He says in a letter to participants:

> I'd like to approach the twin [conference] themes of openness and criticality through a consideration of what I call the interpretive tradition: the tradition, that is, of philosophical hermeneutics. Hermes was the son of Zeus and the god of transitions and boundaries. He acted as the messenger and emissary of Zeus, traversing the space between the mortal and divine, the human world and Mount Olympus. It is in this *in-between* space – the transitional space where meaning is made and boundaries transgressed – that philosophical hermeneutics is located.
>
> (Nixon *et al.*, 2016)

Through the production of texts such as this, it is possible to see how practitioners can position themselves and be accepted by others as knowers of their own practices, regardless of position or rank or capacity in different areas. We all do our best with what we have: the important thing is to ensure that it is our best and not our potential best.

writer, so that your research account is accessible by all, while maintaining the highest forms of research and scholarship. By demonstrating your understanding of the need for these elements within your text, and by showing how you have addressed them, you have automatically shown the realisation of your professional values of accountability, both to others and to the profession. You have done this specifically in response to the challenge of potential professional atrophy: you are keeping the profession vibrant by encouraging it to see itself as always in evolution, towards newer, more contemporary and, therefore, life-enhancing developments.

Towards a view of professionalism as educational research

Further, this focus on demonstrating accountability steers the profession towards an identity that espouses educational values. 'Education' in this sense is applicable to any profession, not only the teaching profession, and broadens the scope of what should count as professionalism. In these days of new public management and corporatisation, professionalism tends increasingly to be narrowly defined as fulfilling the technical needs of the organisation: employees are required to fulfil audits and maintain records of the achievement of targets; they are expected to do research that promotes the interests of the organisation, rather than do blue skies research or engage in thought experiments. Technical rational criteria that include statistical data count more than the educationally and socially oriented qualitative criteria of caring for the other or serving their needs. Further, it leads to a reconsideration of whose interests are being served. Currently, it is the interests of those on the high ground that are served, not those in the small boats bobbing about in the swampy lowlands (see Chapter 1). In the wider sense of more egalitarian ideals, professionalism would be seen to be about fulfilling the needs of service users. Nursing should be for patients, not for

Example 41

Linda Pavitola and Lāsma Latsone work at Liepaja University in Latvia. They are interested in why openness and critique have not been given a high priority in Latvian higher education contexts. They asked twelve faculty members and eleven doctoral-level students why this should be the case. The responses they received were as follows (taken from their notes for a chapter in an edited collection):

> In the Latvian context the main conclusions [for why critique is not given high priority] are as follows:
>
> - For research to be influential in social, professional and political contexts, there is need for a change of personal attitudes towards criticality and openness; changes in ways of thinking are essential;
> - Openness largely depends on researchers' knowledge of foreign languages;
> - Research quality is influenced by time and money;
> - The principles of openness and criticality are often left out of research institution strategies – a research culture needs to be developed that includes themes of communication and research ethics;
> - Quantitative indicators are seen as more important than qualitative ones;
> - There is a lack of prestigious local journals and publications at national level.
>
> It is always important critically to evaluate the usefulness of a research study, the significance of the publication and whether research results are disseminated meaningfully. Holistic research that is open and critical requires teamwork and close collaboration between academics themselves, between academics and University administration, and between academics and students. In the Latvian educational research context we definitely lack a culture of reflection and discussion, critical analysis, and purposeful progress towards achieving the research goals relevant to the University's strategy. Thus, openness and criticality become keywords for conducting valid and internationally legitimated research.
>
> (Pavitova and Latsone, 2016)

the profession; dentistry should be for people who care for their teeth, and landscape gardening should be for people who wish to enjoy beautiful gardens. Recall Habermas's ideas that a system created by people can be recreated by those same, or other, people. In terms of the arguments explored here, by doing your research, you can contribute to this critique and reconceptualisation of your own profession, and, through the publication of your text, you can inspire others to do the same (see Example 41 on page 181).

However, achieving this scenario can be difficult. It means primarily that so-called 'ordinary' practitioners need to engage with their own learning and encourage others to do the same. They need to appreciate that learning is to do with education, and that they are capable themselves of exercising their educational influence in the learning of others. By 'exercising one's educational influence in others' learning' I am not referring to a sinister kind of influence. I take the view, as expressed throughout, that we are all born with the capacity to think for ourselves as part of our genetic inheritance as humans. This capacity allows us to listen to and accept only those messages that are appropriate for our own thinking and contexts: the first step in doing this is to read practitioners' accounts of how they have conducted and theorised their practices. This means that you need to write and publish your work so that it can be accessed by others in your profession, who will see what you have achieved and will be inspired to do the same.

Introducing this critique from the practice setting shows how practitioners can take the lead in knowledge development, which can then lead to their greater participation in defining directions for the profession to take. It also decreases the danger of the profession being directed, as is currently the practice, by small elitist groups whose focus is on securing and maintaining organisational power for themselves. It shows that practice-led approaches are core to defining a coherent, educational model of professionalism that has significant potentials for the flourishing of all members of an organisation.

THE POLITICAL SIGNIFICANCE OF YOUR WRITING

Consider now the potential political significance of your text. Also be aware that, once you enter the realm of the political, you have entered into discourses concerning power.

Different people define the idea of power differently. The view I am committed to is drawn from the work of Hannah Arendt (1958). She says that power is not a thing or the property of an individual that can pass from one person to another so much as what happens when people work together to achieve negotiated goals. Power happens in the interaction, a dynamic, invisible force that permeates a system and filters its way through the cracks of human interactions. Further, the more that people work together, the greater their strength. This process can be seen through, for example, social networking, where groups of people can interconnect in a second. It needs to be remembered, however, that people can use collaboration for different purposes, for social good or social harm. People can come together to find ways of realising their imperialist commitments as much as their democratic ones.

Now, consider the question raised by Chomsky (2000; see Chapter 3, page 65): 'If this explains how things work, how do we account for why they work as they do?' I am suggesting here that the two parts of the question are directly relevant to you. First, you can produce descriptions and explanations of your work in the form of your personal theory of practice: this amounts to 'explaining how things work'. Second, you can show how your theory of practice is rooted in existing systems, with the potential to influence the transformation of those existing systems into new systems that better suit new forms of social evolution: this amounts to 'accounting for why they work as they do'. You can influence systems through researching different ways of doing things and making your findings public, for others to consider adopting or adapting them to their own situations. In this way, your research assumes a new purpose: you can influence systems to point the way for future directions for the field. You do all this by creating knowledge with others and producing texts to show what you have done and what its significance could be for others' learning and actions.

However, if this is what you are trying to do, the question now arises, what do you need to know in order to do so? What kinds of knowledge will best suit your purposes?

I have said throughout that factual knowledge and propositional theory are currently the most valued forms of knowledge in academic contexts. Procedural knowledge is also valued. Practical knowledge is not as valued, and personal knowledge is often dismissed as irrelevant. Ironically (and a reminder of the words of Schön, 1995), this situation is often contradictory to real-world practical experience, where procedural, practical and personal knowledge are as essential as factual knowledge in helping people live productive and fulfilling lives.

I am now suggesting that doing action research with others enables you also to come to know in new ways, both conceptually and practically. Noffke (2009), too, says that action research may be seen as 'a distinctive way of knowing'. Through researching your writing practices, you have learned to produce texts that use those same distinctive ways of knowing to communicate what you are doing more effectively than conventionalist forms of writing.

This means that, through the process, you have developed 'knowledge why': you know why you wish to do things – in this case, in relation to the business of influencing systems – and you can show how this knowledge comes only through working with others (see Example 42 on page 184).

Developing her theme (see above) about how action research may represent a distinctive way of knowing, Noffke continues: 'This point is directly related to whether action research is seen as producing knowledge for others to use, or whether it is primarily as a means for professional development' (2009: 10). This point is relevant to the issue of influencing systems. You are producing knowledge for others to use.

Example 42

Josephine Bleach is director of the Early Learning Initiative (ELI), a community-based educational project in the National College of Ireland (NCI). A core feature of the initiative is that the learning from its action research into the nature of early learning is drawn from collaboration with local people. Its findings are also shared with local, national and international audiences. Josephine writes about the importance of such collaborative practices, as follows:

> If action research is to influence practice, policy and theory, the learning from the process needs to be shared with others. This requires the development of thoughtful and targeted dissemination strategies (Patton and Horton, 2009), which will influence thinking in the public sphere (McNiff, 2010). Understanding the different audiences and the context in which they operate is critical. This chapter [outlines] how evidence of outcomes and impact is used at regular intervals to keep stakeholders, policy makers and funders interested, informed and involved in ELI.
>
> ELI is an integral part of NCI's mission to 'change lives through education'. As a third level institution, NCI is a potent symbol in its local community, providing pre-school, primary and second level students and their families with a visual reminder that they have a right to third level education and that with support it is within their reach (ELI, 2013; Bleach, 2013). Through ELI, NCI supports children and their families as they progress into and through the education system and onto third level.
>
> Sharing learning is at the heart of ELI's action research process and mission. As the 'bridge' between different interest groups (Elliott, 2010), ELI engages in a disciplined and structured way with a range of local, national and international stakeholders on issues of mutual interest. These opportunities enable all involved to create and share knowledge; learn from each other's experience and find solutions to common problems (NCSL, 2002). Having to structure our practices and implicit theories into a coherent explicit theory of practice, which others can understand and relate to, has increased our reflective, relational and representational knowledge (Park, 1999, 2001). This, in turn, has increased our capacity, individually and collectively, to produce results we truly care about (Senge and Scharmer, 2001) and to contribute to the growing library of knowledge resources [a knowledge base] that inform policy and practices in Ireland.
>
> (Bleach, 2016)

This idea is also relevant to Eikeland's (2006) ideas about the need to transform communities of practice into communities of enquiry, outlined in Chapter 8. I suggested there that the form of learning conducted within, and the form of knowledge emerging from, those communities have to be reciprocal and mutually beneficial. We learn from others in our contemporary, horizontal relationships through space, and also from the experience of others who have gone before, through the vertical relationships of time. Through reading those accounts of practice we can see where people were successful, what contributed to their success, and why, from time to time, they had to walk away. We learn from these stories. The point then arises, how do we tell new stories of our own experiences and pass them on, for future generations to learn from what we have done and learned? This then reinforces the need for a new knowledge base, constructed in the present for the future.

Developing a knowledge base for a community of educational enquiry

I am arguing for a new knowledge base of professional practices, grounded in the ideas of communities where all participants enquire into their own practices. Such a knowledge base would comprise the spoken and written texts of the community, as a record of people's thinking at that particular time. The texts produced would provide a record to show how traditions developed within the community that reflected its values at that time. They would also show how new directions for the community were imagined, and suggestions were made for how those recommendations could be implemented, while incorporating potentially new, emergent values orientations.

The realisation of this idea is not simply aspirational; it is happening even as I write. At the time of finalising this chapter, I am on a ship heading for Northern Norway, where I hope to work with a group of higher education healthcare practitioners with the aim of compiling a collection of papers for journal publication. Over the last two days, while on this voyage, colleagues and I have been discussing how we can organise the experiences from our work together in Cambodia for publication as a book. Last week, I was in the UK, where I conducted writing workshops with a group of work-based trades professionals who are writing their portfolios for professional accreditation. Next month, I am giving a talk in South America at a conference for new career researchers from across the professions, who are keen to write up their work as papers and books. And so on, into the future. I am enormously privileged to work with colleagues around the world who are doing fabulous work in their own workplaces and writing up their accounts of practice for publication.

You can and should do the same. There is nothing to stop you. If you are anxious about writing, consider yourself a member of the millions-strong club of researchers who are also anxious about writing. But there is nothing for it but to have a go. If you do not, the penalties are high. If you do not, you will step to one side and continue to allow elites to monopolise the field by default, and thereby perpetuate a view that only elites can write. This is, of course, not the case: anyone can write. It takes work, but it is doable. All you have to do is start writing, and practise, practise and practise again.

Time is not on your side. While you are sitting there feeling anxious, those elites who have much to lose by relinquishing their grip on the knowledge base are also working away in their own corners to maintain power through publications. Some of them also believe they cannot write, but they get on with trying, for they have much to lose. The idea of a battle of words takes on new meaning. It is about who can produce the right words and to what effect, as well as about becoming sufficiently political to know how to get words published in places where they will be read.

There is nothing to stop you. Have faith in the work of your words. Have faith in your own work and find ways to let your voice be heard. Write, and see what happens.

Do a thought experiment. Go to the *Chicago Tribune* hallway and read the words:

> *A good newspaper, I suppose, is a nation talking to itself.*
> – Arthur Miller, 20th century American playwright.

Something similar may be said of a good report or dissertation: it is, I suppose, a community of educational enquiry talking to itself.

Become part of it and see.

Summary

This chapter has proposed some ideas about the potential significance of your writing. It makes the point throughout that writing is one of your most powerful assets, to be used for your own and other people's benefit, and for political purposes in the world. Producing a text may be seen as a form of doing educational research that has implications for the transformation of the existing knowledge base into a new one that shows the amazing opportunities for social good when committed action researchers come together with political intent.

Chapter 10 offers some ideas about how you might do this.

Chapter 10

Where now?

So, where now, now that you have written your text and made sure it meets all the requirements? What do you do next?

You have options. You can say, 'Thank goodness that's over', and resume your normal working life. Many people do this, at least for a day or so, and some for much longer. Or you can say, 'Now, how do I use these wonderful talents I have discovered and developed? How do I find opportunities to disseminate my work and develop new work?'

This second option is the one that will fully vindicate all the effort you have put in, and that will achieve maximum benefit for others from what you have done. Here are some ideas about how you can develop and use your work and talents.

WRITING FOR YOURSELF

You can continue to write for your studies. If you have developed ideas and capacity in writing for, say, one assignment, you can use the same assets for the next. It would be good to keep a learning journal to record your impressions and learning from the experience and use these on an ongoing basis. Writing tends to have an incremental effect: as you develop capacity in writing, ideas begin to generate new ideas more rapidly. You also develop editorial capacity, in that you begin to become your own best critic and see your writing through new eyes. It is an exciting process, because you begin to watch out for things you did not see before. You become good at seeing links and connections in everything. Patterns begin to emerge, and you can get ideas from new reading to use in your work.

You also begin to improve your reading capacity and look out for new themes in other texts. Often, you begin to see gaps in your understanding of events and start reading in greater depth on a particular topic, or develop your range into other areas and disciplines. Don't forget novels and news-papers and fanzines. All texts serve to help you to write and develop capacity for other areas. Writing and reading become part of your daily routines, and your creativity begins to develop exponentially. Once you begin to learn how to write and develop capacity, life becomes new, because now you rightly see yourself as a writer, with a future in writing.

WRITING FOR OTHERS

You should now begin to disseminate your work for others to use. You can disseminate your work through your personal channels. You can post your work on your own website, if you have one, and explain its history and rationale to those who access it, or put it on someone else's. In this way, others can learn from what you have achieved and adopt or adapt your ideas to their practices. You can develop a blog or other means of talking with people. Use your writing to its maximum effect. You could even write a blog about the experience of writing. If learning to improve your writing has demanded a lot of intellectual and emotional energy from you, just think of how other people react, and how you can help them learn from your experience.

You can also benefit from other people's feedback on your work. Invite comment on your texts and use it to improve new writing. It is amazing how much you can improve existing skills through getting and using critical feedback, both on the substantive issues about which you are writing and on the more technical matters of the production of your text. Most people are happy to respond to requests for critical feedback, and you can build up a group of critical writers through online media and social networking. These can develop into active self-help writing groups.

I have seen this happen among working people who are studying part time for their degrees, and I encourage them to develop the practice. I once supported a cohort of twelve working people for their master's degrees, and we set up such an online writing group. It had several unexpected knock-on effects. First, participants benefited, because the feedback they offered one another appeared to hone their skills as editors, which had a superb effect on their own writing. Perhaps, once you begin to critique other people's work, you bring the same critical perspectives to your own. Second, the group benefited, because the members were able to develop their own texts through the critical feedback they received from the others. Third, the entire experience of working as a critical group seemed to raise capacity for critique among all, and it became part of the group culture.

You can do the same. It would be beneficial also to maintain a record of work, so that you can monitor the development and see new possibilities at every turn.

WRITING FOR THE WORLD

At this point, consider publishing your work through regular publication channels, perhaps as articles or as books. Everyone has to start somewhere, and now is your chance. You can find a lot of advice about how to do this in McNiff (2014). There are different kinds of journal: some are written for specific subject matters for a profession; others have a more generalist appeal. Search online or your library database, consult your librarian or your critical friends and find out what is available. Have a go. No one ever found they couldn't do something until they tried, and often people are pleasantly surprised when they find out that they can do it and are actually good at it. Write and produce essays and texts and send them to publishers. Try writing a book. It need not be a highly sophisticated book at first, and you can build capacity over time as you become more confident. Have a look on publishers' websites and see what they need. Most editors are happy to discuss ideas and will give you a lot of support in developing your work. Contact them and see what your options are. Editors are always on the lookout for new authors, so don't be hesitant about having a go.

Of course, this all takes energy and commitment, and it is much easier to sit back and tell yourself that you won't succeed, so there is no use trying. It is much more difficult, and much more fun, to begin to look for opportunities where you can explore ideas and develop your range. There is nothing to lose, and you don't need to tell anyone, so no one will know what you are doing. But just imagine the pleasure and excitement when an editor contacts you and says they would like to develop a conversation with you about producing a text. There is nothing quite like it. Yes, it will take time and energy, but you have that. No one has more than 24 hours in a day. It is an individual's choice what to do with those 24 hours. If you choose to use them to advantage and produce a text from which others can benefit, then you should have a go. You have nothing to lose and everything to gain. Every successful writer had to begin at the bottom and learn the job on the job.

Everyone benefits. You learn how to develop your capacity as a writer, and others learn through reading what you produce. You will not know what you can achieve until you try. Rather than remaining a consumer of other people's work, aim to become a producer of your own and find ways of developing this wonderful talent called writing. It will serve you for life, and others will benefit.

Learn to write with your own pen. Use your voice to tell the truth as you see it. If we all did this, the world would be a better place. Corporate power would find it had a new critical voice to contend with; the academy would find it had a new authority in its midst who has something valuable to contribute.

You have a voice; use it. You have a pen; use it. You have talent; don't waste it, but use it for your own and others' benefit. You can influence millions of lives through your writing. The world is waiting for your text. Take your computer or pen and paper with you on the journey, and don't hold back. Have faith in your own words and find and use them.

A whole new world is there for the exploring. Create a new road: write your text.

References

al-Fugara, S. (2010) 'Developing inclusion in schools: How do I integrate students with additional educational needs into mainstream schooling?' Paper in Tribal and J. McNiff (eds) *Teacher Enquiry Bulletin: Action Research for Teachers in Qatar.* Qatar: Supreme Education Council. Available online at www.jeanmcniff.com/qatar.asp (accessed 27 August 2015).

Al-Hajri, S. H. (2015), Available at: www.jeanmcniff.com/userfiles/file/qatar/Qatar_Action_Research_booklet_email.pdf (accessed 23 August 2015).

al-Tikriti, N. (2010) 'Negligent mnemocide and the shattering of Iraqi collective memory', in R. Baker, S. Ismael and T. Ismael (eds) *Cultural Cleansing in Iraq.* London: Pluto Press, pp. 93–115.

Andrews, R. and England, J. (2012) 'New forms of dissertation', in R. Andrews, E. Borg, S. Boyd Davis, M. Domingo and J. England (eds) *The SAGE Handbook of Digital Dissertations and Theses.* London: Sage, pp. 31–46.

Appadurai, A. (2006) 'The right to research', *Globalizations, Societies & Education,* 4 (2): 167–77.

Arendt, H. (1958) *The Human Condition.* Chicago, IL: Chicago University Press.

Arendt, H. (1990) *On Revolution.* London: Penguin.

Argyris, C. and Schön, D. (1978) *Organisational Learning: A theory of action perspective.* Reading, MA: Addison Wesley.

Argyris, C. and Schön, D. (1995) *Organisational Learning II: Theory, method and practice.* New York: Financial Times/Prentice-Hall.

Aston, S. (2008) Academic Paper, Module 7, MA PVP programme, St Mary's University College, Twickenham, UK.

Baldacci, D. (2015), Available at: www.writingclasses.com/WritingResources/AuthorAdviceDetail.php/author_id/175155 (accessed 29 March 2015).

Barnes, P. (2009) 'Leadership is about relationship'. Module 6 of Master's 'Practitioner research and knowledge transfer' programme. St Mary's University College, Twickenham, UK (off-campus programme delivered in Khayelitsha, South Africa).

Barrett, M. and Whitehead, J. (1985) 'Supporting teachers in their classroom research'. Working paper, University of Bath, School of Education.

Barthes, R. (1970) *S/Z.* New York: Hill & Wang.

Bassey, M. (1999) *Case Study Research in Educational Settings.* Buckingham, UK: Open University Press.

Bateson, G. (1972) *Steps to an Ecology of Mind.* New York: Dutton.

Bateson, G. (2002) *Mind and Nature: A necessary unity.* Cresskill, NJ: Hampton Press.

Bell, J. (2005) *Doing Your Research Project* (4th edn). Maidenhead, UK: Open University Press.

Bell, T. and Penney, D. (2004) 'PlaySMART: Developing thinking and problem solving skills in the context of the National Curriculum for Physical Education in England', in J. Wright, D. Macdonald and L. Burrows (eds) *Critical Inquiry and Problem Solving in Physical Education*. London: Routledge, pp. 49–61.

Benner, P. (1984) *From Novice to Expert: Excellence and power in clinical nursing practices*. Menlo Park, CA: Addison-Wesley.

Benner, P., Sutphen, M., Leonard, V. and Day, L. (2010) *Educating Nurses: A call for radical transformation*. San Francisco, CA: Jossey-Bass.

Bereiter, C. and Scardamalia, M. (1987) *The Psychology of Written Composition*. Hillsdale, NJ: Lawrence Erlbaum.

Berger, J. (1972) *Ways of Seeing*. London: Penguin.

Bergson, H. (1998) *Creative Evolution*. Mineola, NY: Dover. (Originally published in 1911).

Berlin, I. (1969) *Four Essays on Liberty*. London: Oxford University Press.

Biko, S. (1987) *I Write What I Like*. Oxford, UK: Heinemann Educational.

Bishop, G. (2015) 'Storytelling as pedagogy for management development: what does my research tell me about my own teaching practice?' Paper presented at the Fifth International Conference on Value and Virtue in Practice-Based Research, Faculty of Education and Theology, York St John University, York, UK.

Blamey, A. and Mackenzie, M. (2007) 'Theories of change and realistic evaluation: Peas in a pod or apples and oranges?', *Evaluation*, 13 (4): 439–55.

Bleach, J. (2013) 'Community action research: Providing evidence of value and virtue', in J. McNiff (ed.) *Value and Virtue in Practice-Based Research*. Poole, UK: September Books, pp. 17–32. Available online at www.septemberbooks.com/valueand virtue.asp (accessed 27 August 2015).

Bleach, J. (2016, in preparation) 'Sharing the learning from community action research', in J. McNiff (ed.) *Values and Virtues in Higher Education Research*. Abingdon, UK: Routledge.

Boden, M. (1992) *The Creative Mind*. London: Abacus.

Bolton, G. (2010) *Reflective Practice: Writing and professional development* (3rd edn). London: Sage.

Booth, T. and Ainscow, M. (2000) *Index on Inclusion*. Bristol, UK: Centre for Inclusive Education.

Bourdieu, P. (1990) *The Logic of Practice*. Cambridge, UK: Polity.

Boyce, M. E. (1996) 'Organisational story and storytelling: A critical review', *Journal of Organizational Change Management*, 9 (5): 5–26.

Boyer, E. (1990) *Scholarship Reconsidered: Priorities of the professoriate*. Lawrenceville, NJ: Carnegie Foundation for the Advancement of Teaching.

Branson, C., Franken, M. and Penney, D. (in preparation) 'Reconceptualising middle leadership in higher education: A transrelational approach', in J. McNiff (ed.) *Values and Virtues in Higher Education Research*. Abingdon, UK: Routledge.

Brown, J. S. and Duguid, P. (2000) *The Social Life of Information*. Boston, MA: Harvard Business School Press.

Buber, M. (1937) *I and Thou*. Edinburgh, UK: Clark.

Buber, M. (2002) *Between Man and Man*. London: Routledge.

Bullough, R. and Pinnegar, S. (2004) 'Thinking about the thinking about self-study: An analysis of eight chapters', in J. J. Loughran, M. L. Hamilton, V. K. LaBoskey and T. Russell (eds) *International Handbook of Self-Study of Teaching and Teacher-Education Practices*. Dordrecht, Netherlands: Kluwer Academic.

Bunn, M. (2011) 'How to read like a writer', essay in *Writing Spaces: Readings on Writing, Vol. 2*. San Francisco, CA: Parlor Press. Available under the Creative Commons License online at http://writingspaces.org/bunn–how-to-read-like-a-writer (accessed 15 June 2015).

Butler-Kisber, L. (2010) *Qualitative Inquiry*. Los Angeles, CA: Sage.

Capone, D. (2011) *Uncle Al Capone*. [No location recorded] Recap Publishing.

Capra, F. (1996) *The Web of Life*. London: HarperCollins.

Capra, F. (2002) *The Hidden Connections: A science for sustainable living*. London: HarperCollins.

Carr, W. and Kemmis, S. (1986) *Becoming Critical: Education, knowledge and action research*. London: Falmer.

Carpenter, J. (2015), Available at: www.jeanmcniff.com/york-st-john-university.asp (accessed 18 May 2015).

Carroll, L. (1994) *Through the Looking Glass*. London: Penguin Popular Classics. (Originally published in 1872).

Chesbrough, H. (2006) *Open Innovation: The new imperative for creating and profiting from technology*. Boston, MA: Harvard Business School.

Chomsky, N. (1965) *Aspects of the Theory of Syntax*. Cambridge, MA: MIT Press.

Chomsky, N. (1986) *Knowledge of Language*. New York: Praeger.

Chomsky, N. (1991) *Media Control: The spectacular achievements of propaganda*. New York: Seven Stories Press.

Chomsky, N. (2000) *New Horizons in the Study of Language and Mind*. Cambridge, MA: Cambridge University Press.

Chomsky, N. (2002) *Pirates and Emperors, Old and New*. London: Pluto.

Collin, S. and Karsenti, T. (2011) 'The collective dimension of reflective practice: The how and why', *Reflective Practice: International & Multidisciplinary Perspectives*, 12 (4): 569–81.

Collins, J. (2010) *Bring on the Books for Everybody*. Durham, NC: Duke University Press.

Cope, B. and Kalantzis, M. (2000) *Multiliteracies: Literacy learning and the design of social futures*. London: Routledge.

Crawshaw, S. and Jackson, J. (2010) *Small Acts of Resistance*. New York: Sterling.

Creswell, J. W. (2003) *Research Design: Qualitative, quantitative and mixed methods approaches* (2nd edn). Thousand Oaks, CA: Sage.

Creswell, J. W. (2007) *Qualitative Inquiry & Research Design*. Thousand Oaks, CA: Sage.

Cunliffe, A. (2002) 'Reflexive dialogical practice in management learning', *Management Learning*, 33 (1): 3–61.

Cunliffe, A. (2004) 'On becoming a critically reflexive practitioner', *Journal of Management Education*, 28 (4): 407–26.

Davis, V. (2014) *Reinventing Writing: The 9 tools that are changing writing, teaching, and learning forever*. New York: Routledge.

de Certeau, M. (1984) *The Practice of Everyday Life*. Berkeley, CA: University of California Press.

Department of Education and Science [DES] (1991) *Physical Education for Ages 5 to 16*. London: DES.

Dewey, J. (1963) *Experience and Education*. New York: Collier.

Divakaruni, C. (2003) 'New insights into the novel? Try reading three hundred', in *Writers on Writing, Vol. II: More collected essays from The New York Times*. New York: Henry Holt and Company, pp. 37–41.

Doxtader, E. (2009) *With Faith in the Work of Words*. Claremont, South Africa: David Philip.

Dweck, C. (2006) *Mindset: The new psychology of success*. New York: Ballantine.

Dyrberg, T. (1997) *The Circular Structure of Power*. London: Verso.

Early Learning Initiative (ELI). (2013) *Annual Report 2013–14*. Dublin, Ireland: National College of Ireland (unpublished).

Eikeland, O. (2006) 'Condescending ethics and action research: An extended review article', *Action Research*, 4 (1): 37–47.

Elliott, J. (1991) *Action Research for Educational Change*. Buckingham, UK: Open University Press.

Elliott, J. (2010) 'Building social capital for educational action research: The contribution of Bridget Somekh', *Educational Action Research*, 18 (1): 19–28.

Ely, M., Vinz, M. and Downing, M. (1997) *On Writing Qualitative Research: Living by words*. London: Falmer Press.

Fawcett, S. E. and Fawcett, A. M. (2011) 'The "living" case: Structuring storytelling to increase student interest, interaction, and learning', *Journal of Innovative Education*, 9 (2): 287–98.

Fitzgerald, R. and Keelan, A. (1994) 'Improving the quality of staff meetings', in J. McNiff and Ú. Collins (eds) *A New Approach to In-Career Development for Teachers in Ireland*. Bournemouth, UK: Hyde, pp. 184–9.

Foucault, M. (1999) *Abnormal: Lectures at the Collège de France 1974–1975* (trans. G. Burchell). New York: Picador.

Freire, P. (1970) *Pedagogy of the Oppressed*. New York: Herder & Herder.

Freire, P. (2005) *Education for Critical Consciousness*. London: Continuum.

Gadamer, H.-G. (2004) *Truth and Method* (trans. J. Weinsheimer and D. G. Marshall; 2nd rev. edn). London and New York: Continuum.

Gärdenfors, P. (2004) 'Conceptual spaces as a framework for knowledge representation', *Mind & Matter*, 2 (2): 9–27.

Gaventa, J. and Horton, B. D. (1981) 'A citizen's research project in Appalachia, USA', *Convergence: An International Journal of Adult Education*, 14 (3): 30–42.

Gee, J. P. (2014) *An Introduction to Discourse Analysis: Theory and method* (4th edn). Abingdon, UK: Routledge.

Gibbons, M., Limoges, C., Nowotny, H., Schwartzman, S., Scott, P. and Trow, M. (1994) *The New Production of Knowledge: The dynamics of science and research in contemporary societies*. London: Sage.

Glavey, C. (2008) 'Helping eagles fly – A living theory approach to student and young adult leadership development', PhD thesis, University of Glamorgan. Available online at www.jeanmcniff.com/items.asp?id=44 (accessed 10 June 2015).

Goethe, J. W. (1957) *Goethes Werke in Zwei Bänden*. Munich: Droemische Verlagsanstalt Th. Knaur Bachf.

Gold, J., Holman, D. and Thorpe, R. (2002) 'The role of argument analysis and storytelling in facilitating critical thinking', *Management Learning*, 33 (3): 371–88.

Gonzalez, J. (2012) 'Ex-offenders prepare for work, and life, at community colleges' [online article], *The Chronicle of Higher Education*, 58 (40). Available online at http://go.galegroup.com.ezproxy.hope.ac.uk/ps/i.do&id=GALE/A295919217&v=2.1 (accessed 22 October 2013).

Graff, G. (2003) *Clueless in Academe*. New Haven, CT: Yale University Press.

Greenwood, D. and Levin, M. (2007) *Introduction to Action Research* (2nd edn). Thousand Oaks, CA: Sage.

Gudjonsson, H. (2011) 'Action research in Iceland: Influences, development and trends.' Paper presented at the First Value and Virtue in Practice-Based Research Annual Conference, Faculty of Education and Theology, York St John University, York, UK.

Gungqisa, N. (2008) 'Practitioner research and knowledge transfer.' Academic paper, Module 6, MA PVP programme, St Mary's University College, Twickenham, UK (off-campus programme delivered in Khayelitsha, South Africa).

Habermas, J. (1975) *Legitimation Crisis*. Boston, MA: Beacon.

Habermas, J. (1976) *Communication and the Evolution of Society*. Boston, MA: Beacon.

Habermas, J. (1987) *The Theory of Communicative Action: Volume 2: The critique of functionalist reason*. Oxford, UK: Polity.

Hayes, J. R. and Flower, L. S. (1980) 'Identifying the organisation of writing processes', in L. W. Gregg and E. R. Steinberg (eds) *Cognitive Processes in Writing*. Hillsdale, NJ: Lawrence Erlbaum.

Helmer, W. J. and Bilek, A. (2004) *The St Valentine's Day Massacre*. Nashville, TN: Cumberland House.

Helyer, R. (2015) *The Work-Based Learning Student Handbook* (2nd edn). London: Palgrave.

Heron, J. (1996) *Cooperative Inquiry: Research into the human condition*. London: Sage.

Herr, K. and Anderson, G. (2005) *The Action Research Dissertation*. New York: Sage.

Hyde, P. (2013) 'Action research for school improvement', in L. Darbey, J. McNiff and P. Fields (eds) *Evidence Based Handbook: Guidance Case Studies*. Dublin, Ireland: National Centre for Guidance in Education.

Hymes, D. H. (1972) 'On communicative competence', in J. B. Pride and J. Holmes (eds) *Sociolinguistics: Selected Readings*. London, UK: Penguin, pp. 269–93.

Jackson, D. (2008) Academic paper, Module 7, MA PVP programme, St Mary's University College, Twickenham, UK.

Judge, M. (2000) 'Using action research as a means of exploring organisational culture', in J. McNiff, F. McNamara and D. Leonard (eds) *Action Research in Ireland*. Poole, UK: September Books, pp. 201–15.

Kemmis, S. (2009) 'Action research as a practice-based practice', *Educational Action Research*, 17 (3): 463–74.

Kleon, A. (2012) *Steal Like an Artist*. New York: Workman.

Kobler, J. (1992) *Capone: The life and world of Al Capone*. New York: Da Capo Press.

Kondo, T. (2015) Working papers. York, York St John University, Faculty of Education and Theology.

Kushner, S. (2000) *Personalising Evaluation*. London: Sage.

Land, E. (2006) 'Tedco – Enterprise in education.' Previously available online at: www.tedco.org/enterpriseineducation/creativity/behaviour/raising_aspirations/index.htm (accessed 13 April 2008).

Lankshear, C. and Knobel, M. (2011) *Literacies: Social, cultural and historical perspectives*. New York: Peter Lang.

Larsson, S. (2008) *The Girl with the Dragon Tattoo*. London: MacLehose Press.

Latsone, L. and Pavitola, L. (2013) 'The value of researching civic responsibility in the context of Latvia', in J. McNiff (ed.) *Value and Virtue in Practice-Based Research*. Poole, UK: September Books, pp. 93–106. Available online at www.september books.com/valueandvirtue.asp (accessed 28 August 2015).

Laws, S., with Harper, C. and Marcus, R. (2003) *Research for Development*. London: Sage.

Leach, T. and Simpson, K. (2011) 'Using email interviews in collaborative research.' Paper presented at the Second Value and Virtue in Practice-Based Research Annual Conference, York St John University, Faculty of Education and Theology, York, UK.

Lewin, K. (1946) 'Action research and minority problems', *Journal of Social Issues*, 2 (4): 34–46.

Lilla, M. (2001) *The Reckless Mind: Intellectuals in politics*. New York: The New York Review of Books.

Loy, D. (2010) *The World Is Made of Stories*. Boston, MA: Wisdom.

Lyotard, J.-F. (1984) *The Postmodern Condition: A report on knowledge*. Manchester, UK: Manchester University Press.

McDonnell, P. and McNiff, J. (2014) *Action Research for Professional Selling*. Farnham, UK: Gower.

McDonnell, P. and McNiff, J. (2015) *Action Research for Nurses*. London: Sage.

MacIntyre, A. (1985) *After Virtue* (2nd edn). London: Duckworth.

McLaughlin, C. and Ayubayeva, N. (2014) '"It is the research of self experience": feeling the value in action research', *Educational Action Research, Special Issue: Value and Virtue in Practice-Based Research* (ed. J. McNiff), 23 (41): 51–67.

McNiff, J. (1984) 'Action research: A generative model for in-service education', *British Journal of Education*, 10 (3): 40–6.

McNiff, J. (1990) 'Writing and the creation of educational knowledge', in P. Lomax (ed.) *Managing Staff Development in Schools: An Action Research Approach*. Clevedon, UK: Multilingual Matters, pp. 52–60.

McNiff, J. (2000) *Action Research in Organisations*. London: Routledge.

McNiff, J. (2002) *Action Research: Principles and practice* (2nd edn). London: Routledge.

McNiff, J. (2010) *Action Research for Professional Development. Concise advice for new and experienced action researchers*. Poole, UK: September Books.

McNiff, J. (2013) *Action Research: Principles and practice* (3rd edn). Abingdon, UK: Routledge.

McNiff, J. (2014) *Writing and Doing Action Research*. London: Sage.

McNiff, J. (2016) *You and Your Action Research Project* (4th edn). Abingdon, UK: Routledge.

Malgas, Z. (2009) Academic paper, Module 7, MA PVP programme, St Mary's University College, Twickenham, UK (off-campus programme delivered in Khayelitsha, South Africa).

Marshall, C. and Rossman, G. B. (2006) *Designing Qualitative Research* (4th edn). Thousand Oaks, CA: Sage.

Mason, J. (2001) *Researching Your Own Practice: The discipline of noticing*. London: Routledge.

Mathien, T. and Wright, D. G. (eds) (2006) *Autobiography as Philosophy*. Abingdon, UK: Routledge.

Medical Research Council [MRC] (2008) 'Developing and evaluating complex interventions: New guidance.' Available online at www.mrc.ac.uk/documents/pdf/complex-interventions-guidance/ (accessed 28 June 2015).

Mee, S., Buckley, A. and Corless, L. (2015) 'They used to thump the patients, they used to drag 'em: The impact of the voice of experts by experience in higher education.' Paper presented at the Fifth International Conference on Value and Virtue in Practice-Based Research, Faculty of Education and Theology, York St John University, York, UK.

Mitroff, I. and Linstone, H. (1993) *The Unbounded Mind: Breaking the chains of traditional business thinking*. New York: Oxford University Press.

Moore, S. and Murphy, M. (2005) *How to Be a Student*. Maidenhead, UK: Open University Press.

Morgan, S. and Dennehy, R. F. (1997) 'The power of organizational storytelling: A management development perspective', *Journal of Management Development*, 16 (7): 494–501.

Mowles, C. (2015) *Managing in Uncertainty*. Abingdon, UK: Routledge.

Mpondwana, M. (2009) Academic Paper, Module 7, MA PVP programme, St Mary's University College, Twickenham, UK (off-campus programme delivered in Khayelitsha, South Africa)..

Murphy, P. (2000) 'Rehabilitating sexual offenders in religious communities', in J. McNiff (ed.) *Action Research in Organisations*. London: Routledge, pp. 154–9.

Murray, R. (2002) *How to Write a Thesis*. Buckingham, UK: Open University Press.

Nally, J. M., Lockwood, S., Ho, T. and Knutson, K. (2014) 'Post-release recidivism and employment among different types of released offenders: A 5-year follow up study in the United States', *International Journal of Criminal Justice Sciences* [official journal of the South Asian Society of Criminology and Victimology (SASCV)], 9 (1): 16–34.

National College for School Leadership (NCSL). (2002) *Why Networked Learning Communities?* Nottingham, UK: National College for School Leadership.

Nixon, J. (2012) *Interpretive Pedagogies for Higher Education: Arendt, Berger, Said, Nussbaum and their legacies*. London: Bloomsbury.

Nixon, J., Buckley, A., Cheng, A., Dymoke, S., Spiro, J. and Vincent, J. (2016, in preparation) 'The "questionableness" of things: Opening up the conversation', in J. McNiff (ed.) *Values and Virtues in Higher Education Research*. Abingdon, UK: Routledge.

Noffke, S. (2009) 'Revisiting the professional, personal and political dimensions of action research', in S. Noffke and B. Somekh (eds) *The SAGE Handbook of Educational Action Research*. London: Sage.

Nonaka, I. and Takeuchi, H. (1995) *The Knowledge-Creating Company*. Oxford, UK: Oxford University Press.

Norbye, B., Edvardsen, O. and Thoresen, A.-L. (2013) 'Bridging the gap between health care education and clinical practice through action research', in J. McNiff (ed) *Value and Virtue in Practice-Based Research*. Poole, UK: September Books, pp. 69–78. Available online at www.septemberbooks.com/valueandvirtue.asp (accessed 28 August 2015).

Nugent, M. (2000) 'How can I raise the level of self-esteem of second year Junior Certificate Programme students and create a better learning environment?' MA dissertation, University of the West of England, Bristol, UK. Available online at www.jeanmcniff.com/items.asp?id=53 (accessed 28 August 2015).

O'Connor, C. (2015) 'Researching my influence and impact on the lives of former offenders: How can I enable them to gain meaningful work or educational qualifications?' Paper presented at the Fifth International Conference on Value and Virtue in Practice-Based Research, Faculty of Education and Theology, York St John University, York, UK.

O'Neill, R. (2006) 'The transformative potentials of ICT for educational theory.' Paper presented as part of the symposium 'How do we explain the significance of the validity of our self-study enquiries for the future of educational research?', British Educational Research Association Annual Conference, University of Warwick, UK, September. Available online at www.jeanmcniff.com/bera-2006.asp (accessed 11 April 2015).

Orwell, G. (2004) *Why I Write*. London: Penguin.

Park, P. (1999) 'People, knowledge and change in participatory research', *Management Learning*, 30 (2): 141–57.

Park, P. (2001) 'Knowledge and participatory research', in P. Reason and H. Bradbury (eds) *Handbook of Action Research, Participative Inquiry and Practice*. London: Sage, pp. 81–90.

Pavitola, L. and Latsone, L. (2016, in preparation) 'Perspectives on Criticality and Openness in Educational Research in the Context of Latvia': Chapter in J. McNiff (ed.) *Values and Virtues in Higher Education Research*. Abingdon: Routledge.

Patton, M. Q. and Horton, D. (2009) *Utilization-Focused Evaluation for Agricultural Innovation* (Institute of Learning and Change (ILAC) Brief No. 22). Rome, Italy: ILAC.

Pearson, J. (2015) Papers for annual review meeting. Faculty of Education and Theology, York St John University, York, UK.

Peha, S. (n.d.) 'What can you say about a book? Ideas and inspiration for improving book talk and book reviews.' Available online at: www.ttms.org/say_about_a_book/read_like_a_writer.htm (accessed 24 August 2015).

Phillips, E. and Pugh, D. (2005) *How to get a PhD* (4th edn). Maidenhead, UK: Open University Press.

Pink, D. (2012) *To Sell Is Human*. New York: Riverhead.

Polanyi, M. (1958) *Personal Knowledge*. London: Routledge & Kegan Paul.

Popper, K. (1945) *The Open Society and Its Enemies: Volume I: Plato*. London: Routledge & Kegan Paul.

QAA (2008) The framework for higher education qualifications in England, Wales and Northern Ireland. Available online at www.qaa.ac.uk/en/Publications/Documents/Framework-Higher-Education-Qualifications-08.pdf (accessed 1 September 2015).

Raelin, J. A. (2008) *Work-Based Learning: Bridging knowledge and action in the workplace*. San Francisco, CA: Jossey-Bass.

Rand, J. (2016, in preparation) 'The emergence of open-logic sense-making: A practitioner-researcher's experience of openness and criticality', in J. McNiff (ed.) *Values and Virtues in Higher Education Research*. Abingdon, UK: Routledge.

Raz, J. (2003) *The Practice of Value*. Oxford, UK: Oxford University Press.

Reason, P. and Bradbury, H. (eds) (2001) *Handbook of Action Research, Participative Inquiry and Practice*. London: Sage.

Reason, P. and Bradbury, H. (eds) (2008) *The SAGE Handbook of Action Research* (2nd edn). London: Sage.

Reason, P. and Rowan, J. (1981) *Human Inquiry: A sourcebook for new paradigm research*. London: Wiley.

Robson, C. (2011) *Real World Research* (3rd edn). London: John Wiley.

Rorty, R. (2003) Interview, in G. Olson and L. Worsham (eds) *Critical Intellectuals on Writing*. Albany, NY: State University of New York Press.

Rowlands, M. (2005) *Everything I Know I Learned From TV*. London: Ebury Press.

Said, E. (1991) *The World, the Text and the Critic*. London: Vintage.

Said, E. (1994) *Representations of the Intellectual: The 1993 Reith Lectures*. London: Vintage.

Said, E. (1997) *Beginnings: Intent and method*. London: Granta.

Savignon, S. (1972) *Communicative Competence: An experiment in foreign language teaching*. Philadelphia, PA: Centre for Curriculum Development.

Savignon, S. (1991) 'Communicative language teaching: State of the art', *TESOL Quarterly*, 25 (2): 261–77.

Schein, E. H. (1992) *Organizational Culture and Leadership* (2nd edn). San Francisco, CA: Joseey-Bass.

Schön, D. (1983) *The Reflective Practitioner: How professionals think in action*. Boston, MA: Basic.

Schön, D. (1995) 'Knowing-in-action: The new scholarship requires a new epistemology', *Change*, November–December: 27–32.

Schön, D. and Rein, M. (1994) *Frame Reflection*. New York: Basic.

Secretary of State for Education and Skills (2005) *Reducing Re-Offending through Skills and Employment*. Norwich, UK: HMSO.

Sen, A. (2007) *Identity & Violence*. London: Penguin.

Senge, P. and Scharmer, O. (2001) 'Community action research: Learning as a community of practitioners, consultants and researchers', in P. Reason and H. Bradbury (eds) *Handbook of Action Research, Participative Inquiry and Practice*. London: Sage.

Sennett, R. (2009) *The Craftsman*. London: Penguin.

Sennett, R. (2011) *The Foreigner: Two essays on exile*. London: Notting Hill Editions.

Sfard, A. (1998) 'On two metaphors for learning and the dangers of choosing just one', *Educational Researcher*, 27 (2): 4–13.

Sharples, M. (1999) *How We Write: Writing as creative design*. London: Routledge.

Sharples, M. and van der Geest, T. (1996) *The New Writing Environment: Writers at work in a world of technology*. London: Springer.

Shosh, J. (2013) 'Re-articulating the values and virtues of Moravian action research', in J. McNiff (ed.) *Value and Virtue in Practice-Based Research*. Poole, UK: September Books, pp. 107–23. Available online at www.septemberbooks.com/valueand virtue.asp (accessed 28 August 2015).

Sikes, P. and Potts, A. (eds) (2008) *Researching Education from the Inside: Investigations from within*. Abingdon, UK: Routledge.

Sinclair, A. (2013) *Doctoral Study Writings*. York, UK: York St John University.

Speedy, J. and Wyatt, J. (2014) *Collaborative Writing as Inquiry*. Newcastle upon Tyne, UK: Cambridge Scholars.

Spinoza, B. (1996) *Ethics*. London: Penguin Books.

Stenhouse, L. (1975) *An Introduction to Curriculum Research and Development*. London: Heinemann.

Stenhouse, L. (1983) 'Research is systematic enquiry made public', *British Educational Research Journal*, 9 (1): 11–20.

Sternberg, R. and Horvath, J. (1999) *Tacit Knowledge in Professional Practice*. Mahwah, NJ: Lawrence Erlbaum.

Stringer, E. (2007) *Action Research* (3rd edn). Los Angeles, CA: Sage.

Talbot, M. (2001) 'The case for physical education', in G. Doll-Tepper and D. Scoretz (eds) *World Summit on Physical Education*. Berlin, Germany: ICSSPE.

Tate, A. (1940) 'We read as writers', *Princeton Alumni Weekly*, 40 (March): 505–6.

Taylor, D. (2000) 'Introducing multi-skilling training programmes for time-served craft persons in a pharmaceutical manufacturing company', in J. McNiff, G. McNamara and D. Leonard (eds) *Action Research in Ireland*. Poole, UK: September Books, pp. 167–87.

Theroux, P. (1986) *Sunrise With Seamonsters*. London: Penguin.

Thoresen, A.-L. (2011) 'Improving mentoring for midwives in clinical practices.' Paper presented at the First International Conference on Value and Virtue in Practice-Based Research, Faculty of Education and Theology, York St John University, York, UK.

Time to Listen (2015), Available at: www.jeanmcniff.com/items.asp?id=76 (accessed 23 August 2015).

Todorov, T. (1990) *Genres in Discourse*. Cambridge, MA: Cambridge University Press.

Torbert, W. (2001) 'The practice of action inquiry', in P. Reason and H. Bradbury (eds) *Handbook of Action Research: Participative inquiry & practice*. London: Sage, pp. 250–60.

van Wyk, C. (ed.) (2007) *We Write What We Like*. Johannesburg, South Africa: Wits University Press.

Vincent, J. (2015) 'Creating inclusive learning environments through dialogue: A case study outlining the use of autistic students' critical autobiographical narratives in informing academic practice'. Paper presented at the Fifth International Conference on Value and Virtue in Practice-Based Research, Faculty of Education and Theology, York St John University, York, UK.

Vygotsky, L. S. (1962) *Thought and Language*. Cambridge, MA: MIT Press.

Walker, R.and Solvason, C. (2014) *Success With Your Early Years Research Project*. London: Sage.

Walliman, N. and Buckler, S. (2008) *Your Dissertation in Education*. London: Sage.

Whitehead, J. (1989) 'Creating a living educational theory from questions of the kind, "How do I improve my practice?"', *Cambridge Journal of Education*, 19 (1): 137–53.

Widdowson, H. (1983) *Learning Purpose and Language Use*. Oxford, UK: Oxford University Press.

Winter, R. (1989) *Learning from Experience*. London: Falmer.

Wittgenstein, L. (1973) *Philosophical Investigations*. London: Wiley-Blackwell.

Wood, K. (1999) *Wondrous Words: Writing and writers in the elementary classroom*. Urbana, IL: National Council of Teachers of English.

Wyatt, J., Gale, K. and Gannon, S. (2011) *Deleuze and Collaborative Writing: An immanent plane of composition*. New York: Peter Lang.

Young, I. M. (2000) *Inclusion and Democracy*. Oxford, UK: Oxford University Press.

Yukl, G. (2006) *Leadership in Organizations* (6th edn). Upper Saddle River, NJ: Pearson-Prentice Hall.

Zinn, H. (2005) *A People's History of the United States: 1492–Present*. New York: Harper Modern Classics.

Index

Taylor & Francis eBooks

Helping you to choose the right eBooks for your Library

Add Routledge titles to your library's digital collection today. Taylor and Francis ebooks contains over 50,000 titles in the Humanities, Social Sciences, Behavioural Sciences, Built Environment and Law.

Choose from a range of subject packages or create your own!

Benefits for you

» Free MARC records
» COUNTER-compliant usage statistics
» Flexible purchase and pricing options
» All titles DRM-free.

Benefits for your user

» Off-site, anytime access via Athens or referring URL
» Print or copy pages or chapters
» Full content search
» Bookmark, highlight and annotate text
» Access to thousands of pages of quality research at the click of a button.

| REQUEST YOUR **FREE** INSTITUTIONAL TRIAL TODAY | **Free Trials Available** We offer free trials to qualifying academic, corporate and government customers. |

eCollections – Choose from over 30 subject eCollections, including:

Archaeology	Language Learning
Architecture	Law
Asian Studies	Literature
Business & Management	Media & Communication
Classical Studies	Middle East Studies
Construction	Music
Creative & Media Arts	Philosophy
Criminology & Criminal Justice	Planning
Economics	Politics
Education	Psychology & Mental Health
Energy	Religion
Engineering	Security
English Language & Linguistics	Social Work
Environment & Sustainability	Sociology
Geography	Sport
Health Studies	Theatre & Performance
History	Tourism, Hospitality & Events

For more information, pricing enquiries or to order a free trial, please contact your local sales team: www.tandfebooks.com/page/sales

 Routledge
Taylor & Francis Group

The home of Routledge books

www.tandfebooks.com